Literary Occasions

V. S. NAIPAUL was born in Trinidad in 1932. He went to England on a scholarship in 1950. After four years at University College, Oxford, he began to write, and since then has followed no other profession. He has published more than twenty books of fiction and non-fiction, including *Half a Life*, *A House for Mr Biswas*, *A Bend in the River* and most recently *The Masque of Africa*, and a collection of correspondence, *Letters Between a Father and Son*. In 2001 he was awarded the Nobel Prize in Literature.

Literary Occasions

ESSAYS

V. S. NAIPAUL

Introduced and edited by Pankaj Mishra

PICADOR

First published 2003 by Alfred A. Knopf and Alfred A. Knopf Canada

First published in Great Britain 2004 by Picador

This edition published 2011 by Picador
an imprint of Pan Macmillan, a division of Macmillan Publishers Limited
Pan Macmillan, 20 New Wharf Road, London N1 9RR
Basingstoke and Oxford
Associated companies throughout the world
www.panmacmillan.com

ISBN 978-0-330-52297-7

Contents

Introduction

IN 1836, a few months before Pushkin died in a duel, the Russian review journal *Telescope* published the first letter in the collection that came to be known as *Philosophical Letters* by the Russian aristocrat and former army officer Pyotr Chaadaev. For some years, the letters, written originally in French, had been circulating secretly among the Westernised Russians in Moscow and St. Petersburg—among the rootless elite that Peter the Great had created in his attempt to make Russia more like Western Europe. But the publication of the first letter in Russian was, in the words of Alexander Herzen, who read it ecstatically while in exile, like "a shot going off in the dark night." It was, later readers would say, the beginning of intellectual life in Russia.

Chaadaev denounced the cultural isolation and mediocrity of Russia; he denounced, too, the intellectual impotence of the Russian elite, of which he was himself a member. "Our memories" he wrote,

> reach back no further than yesterday; we are, as it were, strangers to ourselves. . . . That is but a natural consequence of a culture that consists entirely of imports and imitation. . . . We absorb all our ideas ready-made, and therefore the indelible trace left in the mind by a progressive move-

ment of ideas, which gives it strength, does not shape our
intellect. . . . We are like children who have not been taught
to think for themselves: when they become adults, they have
nothing of their own—all their knowledge is on the surface
of their being, their soul is not within them.

With these lines, Chaadaev made public some intense growing self-doubts among privileged Russians who looked up, out
of long-established habit, to Western Europe for cultural direction but felt painfully alienated from the vast wretched majority
of the Russian people. In a poem written as early as 1824,
Pushkin had made his protagonist wonder if "the truth is somewhere outside him, perhaps in some other land, in Europe, for
instance, with her stable historical order and well-established
social and civic life." For much of the nineteenth century, Turgenev, Tolstoy and Dostoyevsky were to define in diverse and
fruitful ways their own ambivalent relationship with the West as
well as with their semi-derelict society.

ONE OF Pushkin's disciples, Gogol, turned out to be one of the
most influential figures in this great intellectual and spiritual
awakening of Russia. He published his first stories in 1831–32,
four years before the publication of Chaadaev's letter. It was to
these brisk comic sketches about life in the Ukraine that V. S.
Naipaul once compared the stories about the peasant Indian
world of Trinidad written by his father, Seepersad. Naipaul saw
and heard these stories come into being during the first eighteen
years of his life, which he spent in Trinidad; then, for three
years, from 1950 until his father died, he followed their progress
from England. They gave Naipaul not only his literary ambition but also—at a time of poverty and despair in England,
when Naipaul began to write and didn't know how to go on—
its crucial basis.

The stories drew upon Seepersad's experience as a journalist and government official in the Trinidad countryside, where his own family along with other descendants of Indian indentured labourers had re-created a miniature village India. They dealt partly in romance, in that they presented the Hindu world of the peasants as idyllically whole, in which ancient ritual and myth explained and fulfilled all human desires. Although Seepersad based his characters on members of his own extended family, he did not write about their dereliction and pain, and the humiliation he had himself suffered as a young waif. But then, as Naipaul wrote in his foreword to an edition of Seepersad's stories published in 1976, "certain things can never become material. My father never in his life reached that point of rest from which he could look back at his past."

For Naipaul, the comparison with Gogol ended here. Seepersad found his voice as a writer in the last hard years of life in Port of Spain; Gogol found it at the beginning of his career. Seepersad made the long journey away from his peasant origins, discovered a literary vocation through journalism, only to find that he had little to write about; Gogol overcame in his early stories what Chaadaev saw as a shameful intellectual and literary inertia, and then had, as material, "Russia to fall back on and claim."

As Naipaul saw it, Seepersad was inhibited as much by his "formless, unmade society" as by his personal circumstances. For three centuries, the Caribbean island of Trinidad had been a labour camp for the empires of Europe. Slaves and indentured labourers from different parts of Africa and Asia had steadily replaced its original Indian population. As a colonial society, it was even more artificial, fragmented and dependent on the metropolitan West than the Russia Chaadaev described. It was also very small, politically unimportant and geographically isolated from the rest of the world. It wasn't much encountered in print; and, as the first attempts of Naipaul and his father proved, it was very hard to write about.

From the beginning, there was a "mismatch," as Naipaul later wrote in "Reading and Writing" (1998), between his father's "ambition, coming from outside, from another culture, and our community, which had no living literary tradition." As Naipaul himself discovered, reading the literature that Trinidad imported along with the language from England was more confusing than helpful. "Great novelists wrote about highly organized societies. I had no such society; I couldn't share the assumptions of the writers; I didn't see my world reflected in theirs." Wordsworth's daffodil was a "pretty little flower, no doubt; but we had never seen it." Foreign books worked best when they could be adapted to local conditions. Dickens's rain and drizzle had to be turned into tropical downpours. "But no writer, however individual his vision, could be separated from his society"; and the imported books remained alien and incomprehensible.

At the same time, the literature from Europe had an irresistible glamour—the "soft power" of a successful imperial civilization. It obscured direct vision of one's own society. If "to be a colonial," as Naipaul wrote in an early essay titled "East Indian," was "to be a little ridiculous and unlikely, especially in the eyes of someone from the metropolitan country," then to have, as a colonial, literary ambitions was to know an even deeper shame and awkwardness. For, "until they have been written about societies appear to be without shape and *embarrassing*." It was not easy to resist the doubt that the true subjects of literature lay in Europe, in "its stable historical order and well-established social and civic life."

IT WAS this insidious intellectual colonialism that drained Naipaul of "the courage to do a simple thing like mentioning the name of a Port of Spain street." The embarrassment and difficulty seem to have remained even as Naipaul began, after six futile years in England, to free himself of the metropolitan tradition, and found the courage to write about the Port of Spain street he knew. In *Miguel Street* (1959), his first publishable book, which drew from his childhood in Port of Spain, he simplified and suppressed much of his experience. The memory of the characters came from "a tormented time. But that was not how I remembered it. My family circumstances had been too confused; I preferred not to focus on them."

But he had made a start. *Miguel Street* opened up his Trinidad past, which Naipaul hadn't previously thought of as suitable material, and which he began to explore with rapidly increasing confidence. His next three books included what is now seen as the epic of the post-colonial world, *A House for Mr. Biswas* (1961). In *Biswas,* which drew upon his father's stories of rural Trinidad as well as his lifelong quest for security and stability, Naipaul saw most clearly the "completeness and value" of his experience as a child in Trinidad.

But this material was fixed: "It couldn't be added to." Naipaul was still some years away from a fuller awareness of Trinidad's history—the history of genocide, exploitation, misery and neglect—that he would reach while researching *The Loss of El Dorado* (1969). He couldn't yet write a novel about his years in England; and fiction, which functions "best within certain fixed social boundaries," seemed unable to use fruitfully Naipaul's growing knowledge. Travel books about the Caribbean and India promised a release; but once again, free-floating literary ambition came up against fixed literary tradition. For the travel book, Naipaul discovered, was even more inseparably a part of a metropolitan and imperial tradition than the novel.

The English travelers Naipaul sought to emulate—D. H. Lawrence, Aldous Huxley, Evelyn Waugh—"wrote at a time of empire"; they "inevitably in their travel became semi-imperial." He couldn't be that kind of traveller in either the Caribbean or India, the land of his ancestors. He later wrote of his first trip to India in the early 1960s in *The Enigma of Arrival* (1987) that "there was no model for me here in this exploration, neither Forster nor Ackerley, nor Kipling could help." He couldn't assume their poses of detachment and light irony because "to look as a visitor, at other semi-derelict communities in despoiled land . . . was to see, as from a distance, what one's own community might have looked like."

Such unavoidable reminders of his own past—the past he had barely outgrown in the early sixties—made Naipaul a "fearful traveller" in India. But it also forced him to "define myself very clearly to myself": a reckoning with historical and literary location that became a habit with Naipaul and, eventually, the basis for his assessments of other writers as well. His literary and autobiographical essays, which form a companion volume to the close readings of Indian, African and American societies collected in *The Writer and the World* (2002), discuss writers as varied as Kipling, Gandhi, Nirad C. Chaudhuri, Conrad and R. K. Narayan. They depend on particular, often highly original, interpretations of history and invariably turn upon the problems of self-definition: how writers incarnate or reject the deeper assumptions of the societies they belong to and write about; how their chosen literary form reflects or distorts their particular experiences of the world.

FOR NAIPAUL, both the virtues and limitations of Kipling's *Plain Tales from the Hills* derive from the author's membership in the cosy elite club of imperial Anglo-India. "This artificial, complete and homogenous world did not require explanations." It made Kipling's irony subtle and "private," and his prose "allusive, elliptical . . . easy but packed." However, in Naipaul's complex historical analysis, the same parochial Anglo-India that made Kipling's early work possible prevented the growth of self-knowledge among Indians.

In the second half of the nineteenth century, the British in India moved far from the "New Learning" of Europe they had originally represented to modernising Indians. They came to sympathise more with the "unintellectual simplicities of the blue-eyed Pathan" than with the Bangalis discussing Darwin and Mill. "Suburban and philistine," they became indifferent to the Indian aspirations to modernity which fed the nineteenth-century Bengali intellectual renaissance, and whose passing Nirad C. Chaudhuri mourned in *Autobiography of an Unknown Indian* (1951). Not surprisingly, the cultures of India and Britain remained "opposed"; and the shared language—English—only made for more "cultural confusion."

Naipaul saw the "misunderstandings and futility of the Indo-English encounter" and the "intellectual confusion of the new India" reflected in Indian autobiographies, in their lack of physical detail and rigorous self-questioning. The books spoke to him of a society "which has not learned to see and is incapable of assessing itself, which asks no questions because ritual and myth have provided all the answers." Gandhi's "obsession with vows, food, experiments, recurring illness" had turned his autobiography into a "bastard form in which a religious view of life, laudable in one culture, is converted steadily into self-love, disagreeable in another culture."

For Naipaul, the novel in India was another example of a misunderstood and misapplied literary form. As he saw it, the novel developed, and had its greatest masters, in Europe. This was not an accident. The novel had emerged from the complex interplay of such specific historical factors as industrial growth, imperial expansion, mass literacy, widespread secularisation and the rise of the middle class. The form, "so attractive, apparently easy to imitate," was suffused with, as Naipaul wrote in "Reading and Writing," "metropolitan assumptions about society: the availability of a wider learning, an idea of history, a concern with self-knowledge." In post-colonial India, Naipaul found that either the assumptions were "wrong" or the wider learning was "missing or imperfect."

The novelist R. K. Narayan was a "comfort and example" to both Naipaul and his father in attempting the difficult task of writing in English about Indian life. To Naipaul, he "appeared to be writing from within his culture." "He truly possessed his world. It was complete and always there, waiting for him." But that world proved on closer examination by Naipaul to be static. Narayan's characters seemed to Naipaul "oddly insulated from history"—a history of defeat and subjection that was so oppressively present in India that Narayan's fictional world could only reveal itself as "not, after all, as rooted and complete as it appears." As Naipaul saw it, the novel in India, and specifically Narayan, could "deal well with the externals of things," but often "miss their terrible essence."

NAIPAUL HIMSELF had begun with the externals of things, hoping to arrive, through literature, at "a complete world waiting for me somewhere." "I suppose," Naipaul wrote in an essay on Conrad he published in 1974, "that in my fantasy I had seen myself coming to England as to some purely literary region, where, untrammelled by the accidents of history or background, I could make a romantic career for myself as a writer." Instead, a "political panic" had awaited Naipaul out of his stagnant colonial world of Trinidad. To move in the bigger world was, for Naipaul, to know a cruelly fraught imperial history and his own place in it; it was to be exposed to the "half-made societies" that "constantly made and unmade themselves": the anguished realizations that were made more acute, instead of being mitigated, by his choice of a literary vocation in England.

Almost alone among all major writers in English, Conrad seems to have helped Naipaul understand his peculiar situation and predicament: the predicament of the colonial exile who finds himself working in a world and literary tradition shaped by empire. Conrad was "the first modern writer" Naipaul had been introduced to by his father. He initially puzzled Naipaul: "stories, simple in themselves, always seemed at some stage to elude me." Then, there were the simpleminded assumptions Naipaul made. Reading *Heart of Darkness,* he took for granted the "African background—the 'demoralised land of plunder and licensed cruelty.'"

Travel and writing were to later expose this political innocence of the colonial. For Naipaul, the value of Conrad—also an outsider in England, and an experienced traveller in Asia and Africa—came to exist in the fact that he "had been everywhere before me"; that "he had meditated on my world," "the dark and remote places," where men, "for whatever reason, are denied a clear vision of the world."

Naipaul saw Conrad's work as having "penetrated to many corners of the world which he saw as dark." Naipaul called this fact "a subject for Conradian meditation"; "it tells us something," he said, "about our new world." No writer has meditated more consistently on such ironies of history than Naipaul himself, but with a vitality that seems the opposite of Conrad's calm, slightly self-satisfied melancholy. Naipaul appears to be constantly clarifying and deepening the knowledge or experience that seems complete and hardened in Conrad. Taken together, his books not only describe but also enact how he, starting out in one of Conrad's "dark and remote places," moved slowly and fitfully towards a "clear vision of the world." There is no point of rest in this journey, which now seems an ironic reversal of the Conradian journey to the heart of darkness. Each book is a new beginning, which dismantles what has gone before it. This explains the endlessly replayed drama of arrival, and what seems an obsession with writerly beginnings, in Naipaul's writings.

"Half a writer's work," Naipaul wrote in "Prologue to an Autobiography," "is the discovery of his subject." But his own career proves that such a discovery can occupy a writer most of his life and also constitute, at the same time, his work—particularly a writer as uniquely and diversely displaced as Naipaul, who, unlike nineteenth-century Russian writers, had neither a developing literary tradition nor a vast complex country to "fall back on and claim."

To recognise the fragmented aspects of your identity; to see how they enable you to become who you are; to understand what was necessary about a painful and awkward past and to accept it as part of your being—this ceaseless process, the process, really, of remembering, of reconstituting an individual self deep in its home in history, is what much of Naipaul's work has been compulsively engaged in. Proust's narrator in *In Search of Lost Time* defines the same vital link between memory, self-knowledge and literary endeavour when he says that to create a work of art is also to recover our true life and self, and that "we are by no means free, that we do not choose how we shall make it but that it pre-exists and therefore we are obliged, since it is both necessary and hidden, to do what we should have to do if it were a law of nature, that is to say to discover it."

Pankaj Mishra

LITERARY OCCASIONS

Reading and Writing

A Personal Account

> I have *no memory at all*. That's one of the defects of my mind.
> I keep on brooding over what interests me. By dint of exam-
> ining it from different mental points of view I eventually see
> something new in it, and I *alter its whole aspect*. I point and
> extend the tubes of my glasses in all ways, or retract them.
>
> STENDHAL, *The Life of Henry Brulard* (1835)

1

I WAS ELEVEN, no more, when the wish came to me to be a writer; and then very soon it was a settled ambition. The early age is unusual, but I don't think extraordinary. I have heard that serious collectors, of books or pictures, can begin when they are very young; and recently, in India, I was told by a distinguished film director, Shyam Benegal, that he was six when he decided to make a life in cinema as a director.

With me, though, the ambition to be a writer was for many years a kind of sham. I liked to be given a fountain pen and a bottle of Waterman ink and new ruled exercise books (with margins), but I had no wish or need to write anything; and didn't write anything, not even letters: there was no one to write them to. I wasn't especially good at English composition at school; I didn't make up and tell stories at home. And though I liked new books as physical objects, I wasn't much of a reader. I liked a cheap, thick-paged children's book of *Aesop's Fables* that

I had been given; I liked a volume of Andersen's tales I had bought for myself with birthday money. But with other books—especially those that schoolboys were supposed to like—I had trouble.

For one or two periods a week at school—this was in the fifth standard—the headmaster, Mr. Worm, would read to us from *Twenty Thousand Leagues Under the Sea,* from the Collins Classics series. The fifth standard was the "exhibition" class and was important to the reputation of the school. The exhibitions, given by the government, were to the island's secondary schools. To win an exhibition was to pay no secondary-school fees at all and to get free books right through. It was also to win a kind of fame for oneself and one's school.

I spent two years in the exhibition class; other bright boys had to do the same. In my first year, which was considered a trial year, there were twelve exhibitions for the whole island; the next year there were twenty. Twelve exhibitions or twenty, the school wanted its proper share, and it drove us hard. We sat below a narrow white board on which Mr. Baldwin, one of the teachers (with plastered-down and shiny crinkly hair), had with an awkward hand painted the names of the school's exhibition-winners for the previous ten years. And—worrying dignity—our classroom was also Mr. Worm's office.

He was an elderly mulatto, short and stout, correct in glasses and a suit, and quite a flogger when he roused himself, taking short, stressed breaths while he flogged, as though he were the sufferer. Sometimes, perhaps just to get away from the noisy little school building, where windows and doors were always open and classes were separated only by half partitions, he would take us out to the dusty yard to the shade of the saman tree. His chair would be taken out for him, and he sat below the saman as he sat at his big desk in the classroom. We stood around him and tried to be still. He looked down at the little Collins Classic, oddly like a prayer book in his thick hands, and read Jules Verne like a man saying prayers.

Twenty Thousand Leagues Under the Sea wasn't an examination text. It was only Mr. Worm's way of introducing his exhibition class to general reading. It was meant to give us "background" and at the same time to be a break from our exhibition cramming (Jules Verne was one of those writers boys were supposed to like); but those periods were periods of vacancy for us, and not easy to stand or sit through. I understood every word that was spoken, but I followed nothing. This sometimes happened to me in the cinema; but there I always enjoyed the idea of being at the cinema. From Mr. Worm's Jules Verne I took away nothing and, apart from the names of the submarine and its captain, have no memory of what was read for all those hours.

By this time, though, I had begun to have my own idea of what writing was. It was a private idea, and a curiously ennobling one, separate from school and separate from the disordered and disintegrating life of our Hindu extended family. That idea of writing—which was to give me the ambition to be a writer—had built up from the little things my father read to me from time to time.

My father was a self-educated man who had made himself a journalist. He read in his own way. At this time he was in his early thirties, and still learning. He read many books at once, finishing none, looking not for the story or the argument in any book but for the special qualities or character of the writer. That was where he found his pleasure, and he could savour writers only in little bursts. Sometimes he would call me to listen to two or three or four pages, seldom more, of writing he particularly enjoyed. He read and explained with zest and it was easy for me to like what he liked. In this unlikely way—considering the background: the racially mixed colonial school, the Asian inwardness at home   I had begun to put together an English literary anthology of my own.

These were some of the pieces that were in that anthology before I was twelve: some of the speeches in *Julius Caesar;* scattered pages from the early chapters of *Oliver Twist, Nicholas*

Nickleby and *David Copperfield;* the Perseus story from *The Heroes* by Charles Kingsley; some pages from *The Mill on the Floss;* a romantic Malay tale of love and running away and death by Joseph Conrad; one or two of Lamb's *Tales from Shakespeare;* stories by O. Henry and Maupassant; a cynical page or two, about the Ganges and a religious festival, from *Jesting Pilate* by Aldous Huxley; something in the same vein from *Hindoo Holiday* by J. R. Ackerley; some pages by Somerset Maugham.

The Lamb and the Kingsley should have been too old-fashioned and involved for me. But somehow—no doubt because of the enthusiasm of my father—I was able to simplify everything I listened to. In my mind all the pieces (even those from *Julius Caesar*) took on aspects of the fairytale, became a little like things by Andersen, far off and dateless, easy to play with mentally.

But when I went to the books themselves I found it hard to go beyond what had been read to me. What I already knew was magical; what I tried to read on my own was very far away. The language was too hard; I lost my way in social or historical detail. In the Conrad story the climate and vegetation was like what lay around me, but the Malays seemed extravagant, unreal, and I couldn't place them. When it came to the modern writers their stress on their own personalities shut me out: I couldn't pretend to be Maugham in London or Huxley or Ackerley in India.

I wished to be a writer. But together with the wish there had come the knowledge that the literature that had given me the wish came from another world, far away from our own.

2

WE WERE an immigrant Asian community in a small plantation island in the New World. To me India seemed very far away, mythical, but we were at that time, in all the branches of our extended family, only about forty or fifty years out of India. We were still full of the instincts of people of the Gangetic plain, though year by year the colonial life around us was drawing us in. My own presence in Mr. Worm's class was part of that change. No one so young from our family had been to that school. Others were to follow me to the exhibition class, but I was the first.

Mangled bits of old India (very old, the India of the nineteenth-century villages, which would have been like the India of earlier centuries) were still with me, not only in the enclosed life of our extended family, but also in what came to us sometimes from our community outside.

One of the first big public things I was taken to was the *Ramlila*, the pageant-play based on the *Ramayana*, the epic about the banishment and later triumph of Rama, the Hindu hero-divinity. It was done in an open field in the middle of sugar-cane, on the edge of our small country town. The male performers were barebacked and some carried long bows; they walked in a slow, stylised, rhythmic way, on their toes, and with high, quivering steps; when they made an exit (I am going now by very old memory) they walked down a ramp that had been dug in the earth. The pageant ended with the burning of the big black effigy of the demon king of Lanka. This burning was one of the things people had come for; and the effigy, roughly made, with tar paper on a bamboo frame, had been standing in the open field all the time, as a promise of the conflagration.

Everything in that *Ramlila* had been transported from India in the memories of people. And though as theatre it was crude, and there was much that I would have missed in the story, I believe I understood more and felt more than I had done during *The Prince and the Pauper* and *Sixty Glorious Years* at the local cinema. Those were the very first films I had seen, and I had never had an idea what I was watching. Whereas the *Ramlila* had given reality, and a lot of excitement, to what I had known of the *Ramayana*.

The *Ramayana* was the essential Hindu story. It was the more approachable of our two epics, and it lived among us the way epics lived. It had a strong and fast and rich narrative and, even with the divine machinery, the matter was very human. The characters and their motives could always be discussed; the epic was like a moral education for us all. Everyone around me would have known the story at least in outline; some people knew some of the actual verses. I didn't have to be taught it: the story of Rama's unjust banishment to the dangerous forest was like something I had always known.

It lay below the writing I was to get to know later in the city, the Andersen and Aesop I was to read on my own, and the things my father was to read to me.

3

THE ISLAND was small, 1800 square miles, half a million people, but the population was very mixed and there were many separate worlds.

When my father got a job on the local paper we went to live in the city. It was only twelve miles away, but it was like going to another country. Our little rural Indian world, the disintegrating world of a remembered India, was left behind. I never returned to it; lost touch with the language; never saw another *Ramlila*.

In the city we were in a kind of limbo. There were few Indians there, and no one like us on the street. Though everything was very close, and houses were open to every kind of noise, and no one could really be private in his yard, we continued to live in our old enclosed way, mentally separate from the more colonial, more racially mixed life around us. There were respectable houses with verandahs and hanging ferns. But there were also unfenced yards with three or four rotting little two-roomed wooden houses, like the city slave quarters of a hundred years before, and one or two common yard taps. Street life could be raucous: the big American base was just at the end of the street.

To arrive, after three years in the city, at Mr. Worm's exhibition class, cramming hard all the way, learning everything by heart, living with abstractions, having a grasp of very little, was like entering a cinema some time after the film had started and getting only scattered pointers to the story. It was like that for the twelve years I was to stay in the city before going to England. I never ceased to feel a stranger. I saw people of other groups only from the outside; school friendships were left behind at school or in the street. I had no proper understanding of where I was, and really never had the time to find out: all but nineteen months of those twelve years were spent in a blind, driven kind of colonial studying.

Very soon I got to know that there was a further world outside, of which our colonial world was only a shadow. This outer world—England principally, but also the United States and Canada—ruled us in every way. It sent us governors and everything else we lived by: the cheap preserved foods the island had needed since the slave days (smoked herrings, salted cod, condensed milk, New Brunswick sardines in oil); the special medicines (Dodd's Kidney Pills, Dr. Sloan's Liniment, the tonic called Six Sixty-Six). It sent us—with a break during a bad year of the war, when we used the dimes and nickels of Canada—the coins of England, from the halfpenny to the half-crown, to which we automatically gave values in our dollars and cents, one cent to a halfpenny, twenty-four cents to a shilling.

It sent us text books (Rivington's *Shilling Arithmetic*, Nesfield's *Grammar*) and question papers for the various school certificates. It sent us the films that fed our imaginative life, and *Life* and *Time*. It sent batches of *The Illustrated London News* to Mr. Worm's office. It sent us the Everyman Library and Penguin Books and the Collins Classics. It sent us everything. It had given Mr. Worm Jules Verne. And, through my father, it had given me my private anthology of literature.

The books themselves I couldn't enter on my own. I didn't have the imaginative key. Such social knowledge as I had—a faint remembered village India and a mixed colonial world seen from the outside—didn't help with the literature of the metropolis. I was two worlds away.

I couldn't get on with English public-school stories (I remember the curiously titled *Sparrow in Search of Expulsion*, just arrived from England for Mr. Worm's little library). And later, when I was at the secondary school (I won my exhibition), I had the same trouble with the thrillers or adventure stories in the school library, the Buchan, the Sapper, the Sabatini, the Sax Rohmer, all given the pre-war dignity of leather binding, with the school crest stamped in gold on the front cover. I couldn't see the point of these artificial excitements, or the point of detective novels (a lot of reading, with a certain amount of misdirection, for a little bit of puzzle). And when, not knowing much about new reputations, I tried plain English novels from the public library, too many questions got in the way—about the reality of the people, the artificiality of the narrative method, the purpose of the whole set-up thing, the end reward for me.

My private anthology, and my father's teaching, had given me a high idea of writing. And though I had started from a quite different corner, and was years away from understanding why I felt as I did, my attitude (as I was to discover) was like that of Joseph Conrad, himself at the time a just-published author, when he was sent the novel of a friend. The novel was clearly one of much plot; Conrad saw it not as a revelation of human hearts but as a fabrication of "events which properly speaking are *accidents* only." "All the charm, all the truth," he wrote to the friend, "are thrown away by the . . . mechanism (so to speak) of the story which makes it appear false."

For Conrad as for the narrator of *Under Western Eyes*, the discovery of every tale was a moral one. It was for me, too, without my knowing it. It was where the *Ramayana* and Aesop and Andersen and my private anthology (even the Maupassant and the O. Henry) had led me. When Conrad met H. G. Wells, who thought him too wordy, not giving the story straight, Conrad said, "My dear Wells, what is this *Love and Mr. Lewisham* about? What is all this about Jane Austin? What is it all *about*?"

That was how I had felt in my secondary school, and for many years afterwards as well; but it had not occurred to me to say so. I wouldn't have felt I had the right. I didn't feel competent as a reader until I was twenty-five. I had by that time spent seven years in England, four of them at Oxford, and I had a little of the social knowledge that was necessary for an understanding of English and European fiction. I had also made myself a writer, and was able, therefore, to see writing from the other side. Until then I had read blindly, without judgement, not really knowing how made-up stories were to be assessed.

Certain undeniable things, though, had been added to my anthology during my time at the secondary school. The closest to me were my father's stories about the life of our community. I loved them as writing, as well as for the labour I had seen going into their making. They also anchored me in the world; without them I would have known nothing of our ancestry. And, through the enthusiasm of one teacher, there were three literary experiences in the sixth form: *Tartuffe*, which was like a frightening fairytale, *Cyrano de Bergerac*, which could call up the profoundest kind of emotion, and *Lazarillo de Tormes*, the mid-sixteenth-century Spanish picaresque story, the first of its kind, brisk and ironical, which took me into a world like the one I knew.

That was all. That was the stock of my reading at the end of my island education. I couldn't truly call myself a reader. I had never had the capacity to lose myself in a book; like my father, I could read only in little bits. My school essays weren't exceptional; they were only crammer's work. In spite of my father's example with his stories I hadn't begun to think in any concrete way about what I might write. Yet I continued to think of myself as a writer.

It was now less a true ambition than a form of self-esteem, a dream of release, an idea of nobility. My life, and the life of our section of our extended family, had always been unsettled. My father, though not an orphan, had been a kind of waif since his childhood; and we had always been half dependent. As a journalist my father was poorly paid, and for some years we had been quite wretched, with no proper place to live. At school I was a bright boy; on the street, where we still held ourselves apart, I felt ashamed at our condition. Even after that bad time had passed, and we had moved, I was eaten up with anxiety. It was the emotion I felt I had always known.

4

THE COLONIAL government gave four scholarships a year to Higher School Certificate students who came top of their group—languages, modern studies, science, mathematics. The question papers were sent out from England, and the students' scripts were sent back there to be marked. The scholarships were generous. They were meant to give a man or woman a profession. The scholarship-winner could go at the government's expense to any university or place of higher education in the British empire; and his scholarship could run for seven years. When I won my scholarship—after a labour that still hurts to think about: it was what all the years of cramming were meant to lead to—I decided only to go to Oxford and do the three-year English course. I didn't do this for the sake of Oxford and the English course; I knew little enough about either. I did it mainly to get away to the bigger world and give myself time to live up to my fantasy and become a writer.

To be a writer was to be a writer of novels and stories. That was how the ambition had come to me, through my anthology and my father's example, and that was where it had stayed. It was strange that I hadn't questioned this idea, since I had no taste for novels, hadn't felt the impulse (which children are said to feel) to make up stories, and nearly all my imaginative life during the long cramming years had been in the cinema, and not in books. Sometimes when I thought of the writing blankness inside me I felt nervous; and then—it was like a belief in magic—I told myself that when the time came there would be no blankness and the books would get written.

At Oxford now, on that hard-earned scholarship, the time should have come. But the blankness was still there; and the very idea of fiction and the novel was continuing to puzzle me. A novel was something made up; that was almost its definition. At the same time it was expected to be true, to be drawn from life; so that part of the point of a novel came from half rejecting the fiction, or looking through it to a reality.

Later, when I had begun to identify my material and had begun to be a writer, working more or less intuitively, this ambiguity ceased to worry me. In 1955, the year of this breakthrough, I was able to understand Evelyn Waugh's definition of fiction (in the dedication to *Officers and Gentlemen*, published that year) as "experience totally transformed"; I wouldn't have understood or believed the words the year before.

More than forty years later, when I was reading Tolstoy's Sebastopol sketches for the first time, I was reminded of that early writing happiness of mine when I began to see a way ahead. I thought that in those sketches I could see the young Tolstoy moving, as if out of need, to the discovery of fiction: starting as a careful descriptive writer (a Russian counterpart of William Howard Russell, the *Times* correspondent, not much older, on the other side), and then, as though seeing an easier and a better way of dealing with the horrors of the Sebastopol siege, doing a simple fiction, setting characters in motion, and bringing the reality closer.

A discovery like that was to come to me, but not at Oxford. No magic happened in my three years there, or in the fourth that the Colonial Office allowed me. I continued to fret over the idea of fiction as something made up. How far could the making up (Conrad's "accidents") go? What was the logic and what was the value? I was led down many byways. I felt my writing personality as something grotesquely fluid. It gave me no pleasure to sit down at a table and pretend to write; I felt self-conscious and false.

If I had had even a little money, or the prospects of a fair job, it would have been easy then to let the writing idea drop. I saw it now only as a fantasy born out of childhood worry and ignorance, and it had become a burden. But there was no money. I had to hold on to the idea.

I was nearly destitute—I had perhaps six pounds—when I left Oxford and went to London to set up as a writer. All that remained of my scholarship, which seemed now to have been prodigally squandered, was the return fare home. For five months I was given shelter in a dark Paddington basement by an older cousin, a respecter of my ambition, himself very poor, studying law and working in a cigarette factory.

Nothing happened with my writing during those five months; nothing happened for five months afterwards. And then one day, deep in my almost fixed depression, I began to see what my material might be: the city street from whose mixed life we had held aloof, and the country life before that, with the ways and manners of a remembered India. It seemed easy and obvious when it had been found; but it had taken me four years to see it. Almost at the same time came the language, the tone, the voice for that material. It was as if voice and matter and form were part of one another.

Part of the voice was my father's, from his stories of the country life of our community. Part of it was from the anonymous *Lazarillo,* from mid-sixteenth-century Spain. (In my second year at Oxford I had written to E. V. Rieu, editor of the Penguin Classics, offering to translate *Lazarillo.* He had replied very civilly, in his own hand, saying it would be a difficult book to do, and he didn't think it was a classic. I had nonetheless, dur-

ing my blankness, as a substitute for writing, done a full transla-
tion.) The mixed voice fitted. It was not absolutely my own
when it came to me, but I was not uneasy with it. It was, in fact,
the writing voice which I had worked hard to find. Soon it was
familiar, the voice in my head. I could tell when it was right and
when it was going off the rails.

To get started as a writer, I had had to go back to the beginning, and pick my way back—forgetting Oxford and London—to those early literary experiences, some of them not
shared by anybody else, which had given me my own view of
what lay about me.

5

IN MY fantasy of being a writer there had been no idea how I
might actually go about writing a book. I suppose—I couldn't
be sure—that there was a vague notion in the fantasy that once
I had done the first the others would follow.

I found it wasn't like that. The material didn't permit it. In
those early days every new book meant facing the old blankness
again and going back to the beginning. The later books came
like the first, driven only by the wish to do a book, with an intuitive or innocent or desperate grasping at ideas and material
without fully understanding where they might lead. Knowledge
came with the writing. Each book took me to deeper understanding and deeper feeling, and that led to a different way of
writing. Every book was a stage in a process of finding out; it
couldn't be repeated. My material—my past, separated from me
by place as well—was fixed and, like childhood itself, complete;
it couldn't be added to. This way of writing consumed it.
Within five years I had come to an end. My writing imagination
was like a chalk-scrawled blackboard, wiped clean in stages, and
at the end blank again, *tabula rasa*.

Fiction had taken me as far as it could go. There were certain things it couldn't deal with. It couldn't deal with my years in England; there was no social depth to the experience; it seemed more a matter for autobiography. And it couldn't deal with my growing knowledge of the wider world. Fiction, by its nature, functioning best within certain fixed social boundaries, seemed to be pushing me back to worlds—like the island world, or the world of my childhood—smaller than the one I inhabited. Fiction, which had once liberated me and enlightened me, now seemed to be pushing me towards being simpler than I really was. For some years—three, perhaps four—I didn't know how to move; I was quite lost.

Nearly all my adult life had been spent in countries where I was a stranger. I couldn't as a writer go beyond that experience. To be true to that experience I had to write about people in that kind of position. I found ways of doing so; but I never ceased to feel it as a constraint. If I had had to depend only on the novel I would probably have soon found myself without the means of going on, though I had trained myself in prose narrative and was full of curiosity about the world and people.

But there were other forms that met my need. Accident had fairly early on brought me a commission to travel in the former slave colonies of the Caribbean and the old Spanish Main. I had accepted for the sake of the travel; I hadn't thought much about the form.

I had an idea that the travel book was a glamorous interlude in the life of a serious writer. But the writers I had had in mind—and there could have been no other—were metropolitan people, Huxley, Lawrence, Waugh. I was not like them. They wrote at a time of empire; whatever their character at home, they inevitably in their travel became semi-imperial, using the accidents of travel to define their metropolitan personalities against a foreign background.

My travel was not like that. I was a colonial travelling in New World plantation colonies which were like the one I had grown up in. To look, as a visitor, at other semi-derelict communities in despoiled land, in the great romantic setting of the New World, was to see, as from a distance, what one's own community might have looked like. It was to be taken out of oneself and one's immediate circumstances—the material of fiction—and to have a new vision of what one had been born into, and to have an intimation of a sequence of historical events going far back.

I had trouble with the form. I didn't know how to travel for a book. I travelled as though I was on holiday, and then floundered, looking for the narrative. I had trouble with the "I" of the travel writer; I thought that as traveller and narrator he was in unchallenged command and had to make big judgements.

For all its faults, the book, like the fiction books that had gone before, was for me an extension of knowledge and feeling. It wouldn't have been possible for me to unlearn what I had learned. Fiction, the exploration of one's immediate circumstances, had taken me a lot of the way. Travel had taken me further.

6

IT WAS accident again that set me to doing another kind of nonfiction book. A publisher in the United States was doing a series for travellers, and asked me to do something about the colony. I thought it would be a simple labour: a little local history, some personal memories, some word pictures.

I had thought, with a strange kind of innocence, that in our world all knowledge was available, that all history was stored somewhere and could be retrieved according to need. I found now that there was no local history to consult. There were only a few guide books in which certain legends were repeated. The colony had not been important; its past had disappeared. In some of the guide books the humorous point was made that the colony was a place where nothing of note had happened since Sir Walter Raleigh's visit in 1595.

I had to go to the records. There were the reports of travellers. There were the British official papers. In the British Museum there were very many big volumes of copies of relevant Spanish records, dug up by the British government from the Spanish archives in the 1890s, at the time of the British Guiana–Venezuela border dispute. I looked in the records for people and their stories. It was the best way of organising the material, and it was the only way I knew to write. But it was hard work, picking through the papers, and using details from five or six or more documents to write a paragraph of narrative. The book which I had thought I would do in a few months took two hard years.

The records took me back almost to the discovery. They showed me the aboriginal peoples, masters of sea and river, busy about their own affairs, possessing all the skills they had needed in past centuries, but helpless before the newcomers, and ground down over the next two hundred years to nonentity, alcoholism, missionary reserves and extinction. In this manmade wilderness then, in the late eighteenth century, the slave plantations were laid out, and the straight lines of the new Spanish town.

At school, in the history class, slavery was only a word. One day in the school yard, in Mr. Worm's class, when there was some talk of the subject, I remember trying to give meaning to the word: looking up to the hills to the north of the city and thinking that those hills would once have been looked upon by people who were not free. The idea was too painful to hold on to.

The documents now, many years after that moment in the school yard, made that time of slavery real. They gave me glimpses of the life of the plantations. One plantation would have been very near the school; a street not far away still carried the Anglicised French name of the eighteenth-century owner. In the documents I went—and very often—to the city jail, where the principal business of the French jailer and his slave assistant was the punishing of slaves (the charges depended on the punishment given, and the planters paid), and where there were special hot cells, just below the roof shingles, for slaves who were thought to be sorcerers.

From the records of an unusual murder trial—one slave had killed another at a wake for a free woman of colour—I got an idea of the slave life of the streets in the 1790s, and understood that the kind of street we had lived on, and the kind of street life I had studied from a distance, were close to the streets and life of a hundred and fifty years before. That idea, of a history or an ancestry for the city street, was new to me. What I had known had seemed to me ordinary, unplanned, just there, with nothing like a past. But the past was there: in the school yard, in Mr. Worm's class, below the saman tree, we stood perhaps on the site of Dominique Dert's Bel-Air estate, where in 1803 the slave *commandeur,* the estate driver or headman, out of a twisted love for his master, had tried to poison the other slaves.

More haunting than this was the thought of the vanished aborigines, on whose land and among whose spirits we all lived. The country town where I was born, and where in a clearing in the sugarcane I had seen our *Ramlila,* had an aboriginal name. One day in the British Museum I discovered—in a letter of 1625 from the King of Spain to the local governor—that it was the name of a troublesome small tribe of just over a thousand. In 1617 they had acted as river guides for English raiders. Eight years later—Spain had a long memory—the Spanish governor had assembled enough men to inflict some unspecified collective punishment on the tribe; and their name had disappeared from the records.

This was more than a fact about the aborigines. It to some extent altered my own past. I could no longer think of the *Ramlila* I had seen as a child as occurring at the very beginning of things. I had imaginatively to make room for people of another kind on the *Ramlila* ground. Fiction by itself would not have taken me to this larger comprehension.

I didn't do a book like that again, working from documents

alone. But the technique I had acquired—of looking through a multiplicity of impressions to a central human narrative—was something I took to the books of travel (or, more properly, inquiry) that I did over the next thirty years. So, as my world widened, beyond the immediate personal circumstances that bred fiction, and as my comprehension widened, the literary forms I practised flowed together and supported one another; and I couldn't say that one form was higher than another. The form depended on the material; the books were all part of the same process of understanding. It was what the writing career— at first only a child's fantasy, and then a more desperate wish to write stories—had committed me to.

The novel was an imported form. For the metropolitan writer it was only one aspect of self-knowledge. About it was a mass of other learning, other imaginative forms, other disciplines. For me, in the beginning, it was my all. Unlike the metropolitan writer I had no knowledge of a past. The past of our community ended, for most of us, with our grandfathers; beyond that we could not see. And the plantation colony, as the humorous guide books said, was a place where almost nothing had happened. So the fiction one did, about one's immediate circumstances, hung in a void, without a context, without the larger self-knowledge that was always implied in a metropolitan novel.

As a child trying to read, I had felt that two worlds separated me from the books that were offered to me at school and in the libraries: the childhood world of our remembered India, and the more colonial world of our city. I had thought that the difficulties had to do with the social and emotional disturbances of my childhood—that feeling of having entered the cinema long after the film had started—and that the difficulties would blow away as I got older. What I didn't know, even after I had written my early books of fiction, concerned only with story and people and getting to the end and mounting the jokes well, was that those two spheres of darkness had become my subject. Fiction, working its mysteries, by indirections finding directions out, had led me to my subject. But it couldn't take me all the way.

7

INDIA WAS the greater hurt. It was a subject country. It was also the place from whose very great poverty our grandfathers had had to run away in the late nineteenth century. The two Indias were separate. The political India, of the freedom movement, had its great names. The other, more personal India was quite hidden; it vanished when memories faded. It wasn't an India we could read about. It wasn't Kipling's India, or E. M. Forster's, or Somerset Maugham's; and it was far from the somewhat stylish India of Nehru and Tagore. (There was an Indian writer, Premchand [1880–1936], whose stories in Hindi and Urdu would have made our Indian village past real to us. But we didn't know about him; we were not reading people in that way.)

It was to this personal India, and not the India of independence and its great names, that I went when the time came. I was full of nerves. But nothing had prepared me for the dereliction I saw. No other country I knew had so many layers of wretchedness, and few countries were as populous. I felt I was in a continent where, separate from the rest of the world, a mysterious calamity had occurred. Yet what was so overwhelming to me, so much in the foreground, was not to be found in the modern-day writing I knew, Indian or English. In one Kipling story an Indian famine was a background to an English romance; but generally in both English and Indian kinds the extraordinary distress of India, when acknowledged, was like something given, eternal, something to be read only as background. And there were, as always, those who thought they could find a special spiritual quality in the special Indian distress.

It was only in Gandhi's autobiography, *The Story of My Experiments with Truth,* in the chapters dealing with his discovery in the 1890s of the wretchedness of the unprotected Indian labourers in South Africa, that I found—obliquely, and not for long—a rawness of hurt that was like my own in India.

I wrote a book, after having given up the idea. But I couldn't let go of the hurt. It took time—much writing, in many moods—to see beyond the dereliction. It took time to break through the bias and the fantasies of Indian political ideas about the Indian past. The independence struggle, the movement against the British, had obscured the calamities of India before the British. Evidence of those calamities lay on every side. But the independence movement was like religion; it didn't see what it didn't want to see.

For more than six hundred years after 1000 A.D. the Muslim invaders had ravaged the subcontinent at will. They had established kingdoms and empires and fought with one another. They had obliterated the temples of the local religions in the north; they had penetrated deep into the south and desecrated temples there.

For twentieth-century Indian nationalism those centuries of defeat were awkward. So history was re-jigged; ruler and ruled before the British, conqueror and subject, believer and infidel, became one. In the face of the great British power, it made a kind of sense. Still, to promote the idea of the wholeness of India before the British, it was easier for nationalist writers to go very far back, to pre-Islamic days, to the fifth and seventh centuries, when India was for some the centre of the world, and Chinese Buddhist scholars came as pilgrims to Buddhist centres of learning in India.

The fourteenth-century Moroccan Muslim theologian and world traveller Ibn Battuta didn't fit in so easily with this idea of Indian wholeness. Ibn Battuta wished to travel to all the countries of the Muslim world. Everywhere he went he lived on the bounty of Muslim rulers, and he offered pure Arab piety in return.

He came to India as to a conquered Muslim land. He was granted the revenues (or crops) of five villages, then—in spite of a famine—two more; and he stayed for seven years. In the end, though, he had to run. The Muslim ruler in Delhi, Ibn Battuta's ultimate patron, liked blood, daily executions (and torture) on the threshold of his hall of audience, with the bodies left lying for three days. Even Ibn Battuta, though used to the ways of Muslim despots the world over, began to take fright. When four guards were set to watch him he thought his time had come. He had been pestering the ruler and his officials for this and that, and complaining that the ruler's gifts were being soaked up by officials before they got to him. Now, with the inspiration of terror, he declared himself a penitent who had renounced the world. He did a full five-day fast, reading the Koran right through every day of his fast; and when he next appeared before the ruler he was dressed like a mendicant. The renunciation of the theologian touched the hard heart of the ruler, reminded him of higher things, and Ibn Battuta was allowed to go.

In Ibn Battuta's narrative the local people were only obliquely seen. They were serfs in the villages (the property of the ruler, part of the bounty that could be offered the traveller) or simple slaves (Ibn Battuta liked travelling with slave girls). The beliefs of these people had a quaint side but were otherwise of no interest to a Muslim theologian; in Delhi their idols had been literally overthrown. The land had ceased to belong to the local people, and it had no sacredness for the foreign ruler.

In Ibn Battuta it was possible to see the beginnings of the great dereliction of India. To seventeenth-century European travellers like Thomas Roe and Bernier the general wretchedness of the people—living in huts just outside the Mogul palaces—mocked the pretentiousness of the rulers. And for William Howard Russell, reporting in 1858 and 1859 on the Indian Mutiny for *The Times,* and travelling slowly from Calcutta to the Punjab, the land was everywhere in old ruin, with the half-starved ("hollow-thighed") common people, blindly going about their menial work, serving the British as they had served every previous ruler.

Even if I had not found words for it, I had believed as a child in the wholeness of India. The *Ramlila* and our religious rites and all our private ways were part of that wholeness; it was something we had left behind. This new idea of the past, coming to me over the years, unravelled that romance, showed me that our ancestral civilization—to which we had paid tribute in so many ways in our far-off colony, and had thought of as ancient and unbroken—had been as helpless before the Muslim invaders as the Mexicans and Peruvians were before the Spaniards; had been half destroyed.

8

FOR EVERY kind of experience there is a proper form, and I do not see what kind of novel I could have written about India. Fiction works best in a confined moral and cultural area, where the rules are generally known; and in that confined area it deals best with things—emotions, impulses, moral anxieties—that would be unseizable or incomplete in other literary forms.

The experience I had had was particular to me. To do a novel about it, it would have been necessary to create someone like myself, someone of my ancestry and background, and to work out some business which would have taken this person to India. It would have been necessary more or less to duplicate the original experience, and it would have added nothing. Tolstoy used fiction to bring the siege of Sebastopol closer, to give it an added reality. I feel that if I had attempted a novel about India, and mounted all that apparatus of invention, I would have been falsifying precious experience. The value of the experience lay in its particularity. I had to render it as faithfully as I could.

The metropolitan novel, so attractive, so apparently easy to imitate, comes with metropolitan assumptions about society:

the availability of a wider learning, an idea of history, a concern with self-knowledge. Where those assumptions are wrong, where the wider learning is missing or imperfect, I am not sure whether the novel can offer more than the externals of things. The Japanese imported the novel form and added it to their own rich literary and historical traditions; there was no mismatch. But where, as in India, the past has been torn away, and history is unknown or unknowable or denied, I don't know whether the borrowed form of the novel can deliver more than a partial truth, a dim lighted window in a general darkness.

Forty to fifty years ago, when Indian writers were not so well considered, the writer R. K. Narayan was a comfort and example to those of us (I include my father and myself) who wished to write. Narayan wrote in English about Indian life. This is actually a difficult thing to do, and Narayan solved the problems by appearing to ignore them. He wrote lightly, directly, with little social explanation. His English was so personal and easy, so without English social associations, that there was no feeling of oddity; he always appeared to be writing from within his culture.

He wrote about people in a small town in South India: small people, big talk, small doings. That was where he began; that was where he was fifty years later. To some extent that reflected Narayan's own life. He never moved far from his origins. When I met him in London in 1961—he had been travelling, and was about to go back to India—he told me he needed to be back home, to do his walks (with an umbrella for the sun) and to be among his characters.

He truly possessed his world. It was complete and always there, waiting for him; and it was far enough away from the centre of things for outside disturbances to die down before they could get to it. Even the independence movement, in the heated 1930s and 1940s, was far away, and the British presence was marked mainly by the names of buildings and places. This was an India that appeared to mock the vainglorious and went on in its own way.

Dynasties rose and fell. Palaces and mansions appeared and disappeared. The entire country went down under the fire and sword of the invader, and was washed clean when Sarayu [the local river] overflowed its bounds. But it always had its rebirth and growth.

In this view (from one of the more mystical of Narayan's books) the fire and sword of defeat are like abstractions. There is no true suffering, and rebirth is almost magical. These small people of Narayan's books, earning petty sums from petty jobs, and comforted and ruled by ritual, seem oddly insulated from history. They seem to have been breathed into being; and on examination they don't appear to have an ancestry. They have only a father and perhaps a grandfather; they cannot reach back further into the past. They go to ancient temples; but they do not have the confidence of those ancient builders; they themselves can build nothing that will last.

But the land is sacred, and it has a past. A character in that same mystical novel is granted a simple vision of that Indian past, and it comes in simple tableaux. The first is from the *Ramayana* (about 1000 B.C.); the second is of the Buddha, from the sixth century B.C.; the third is of the ninth-century philosopher Shankaracharya; the fourth is of the arrival a thousand years later of the British, ending with Mr. Shilling, the local bank manager.

What the tableaux leave out are the centuries of the Muslim invasions and Muslim rule. Narayan spent part of his childhood in the state of Mysore. Mysore had a Hindu maharaja. The British put him on the throne after they had defeated the Muslim ruler. The maharaja was of an illustrious family; his ancestors had been satraps of the last great Hindu kingdom of the south. That kingdom was defeated by the Muslims in 1565, and its enormous capital city (with the accumulated human talent that had sustained it) almost totally destroyed, leaving a land so impoverished, so nearly without creative human resource, that it is hard now to see how a great empire could have arisen on that spot. The terrible ruins of the capital—still speaking four centuries later of loot and hate and blood and Hindu defeat, a whole world destroyed—were perhaps a day's journey from Mysore City.

Narayan's world is not, after all, as rooted and complete as it appears. His small people dream simply of what they think has gone before, but they are without personal ancestry; there is a great blank in their past. Their lives are small, as they have to be: this smallness is what has been allowed to come up in the ruins, with the simple new structures of British colonial order (school, road, bank, courts). In Narayan's books, when the history is known, there is less the life of a wise and eternal Hindu India than a celebration of the redeeming British peace.

So in India the borrowed form of the English or European novel, even when it has learned to deal well with the externals of things, can sometimes miss their terrible essence.

I too, as a writer of fiction, barely understanding my world—our family background, our migration, the curious half-remembered India in which we continued to live for a generation, Mr. Worm's school, my father's literary ambition—I too could begin only with the externals of things. To do more, as I soon had to, since I had no idea or illusion of a complete world waiting for me somewhere, I had to find other ways.

9

FOR SIXTY or seventy years in the nineteenth century the novel in Europe, developing very fast in the hands of a relay of masters, became an extraordinary tool. It did what no other literary form—essay, poem, drama, history—could do. It gave industrial or industrialising or modern society a very clear idea of itself. It showed with immediacy what hadn't been shown before; and it altered vision. Certain things in the form could be modified or played with later, but the pattern of the modern novel had been set, and its programme laid out.

All of us who have come after have been derivative. We can never be the first again. We might bring new material from far away, but the programme we are following has been laid out for us. We cannot be the writing equivalent of Robinson Crusoe on his island, letting off "the first gun that had been fired there since the creation of the world." That (to stay with the metaphor) is the gunshot we hear when we turn to the originators. They are the first; they didn't know it when they began, but then (like Machiavelli in his *Discourses* and Montaigne in his *Essays*) they do know, and they are full of excitement at the discovery. That excitement comes over to us, and there is an unrepeatable energy in the writing.

The long passage below is from the beginning of *Nicholas Nickleby* (1838). Dickens is twenty-six and at his freshest. The material is commonplace. That is its point. Dickens appears to have just discovered (after Boz and Pickwick and *Oliver Twist*) that everything he sees in London is his to write about, and that plot can wait.

Mr. Nickleby closed an account-book which lay on his desk and, throwing himself back in his chair, gazed with an air of abstraction through the dirty window. Some London houses have a melancholy little plot of ground behind them, usually fenced in by four whitewashed walls, and frowned upon by stacks of chimneys: in which there withers on, from year to year, a crippled tree, that makes a show of putting forth a few leaves late in autumn when other trees shed theirs, and, drooping in the effort, lingers on, all crackled and smoke-dried, till the following season. . . . People some-times call these dark yards "gardens"; it is not supposed that they were ever planted, but rather that they are pieces of unreclaimed land, with the withered vegetation of the original brick-field. No man thinks of walking in this desolate place, or of turning it to any account. A few hampers, half-a-dozen broken bottles, and such-like rubbish, may be thrown there, when the tenant first moves in, but nothing more; and there they remain until he goes away again: the damp straw taking just as long to moulder as it thinks proper: and mingling with the scanty box, and stunted ever-browns, and broken flowerpots, that are scattered mournfully about—a prey to "blacks" and dirt.

It was into a place of this kind that Mr. Ralph Nickleby gazed.... He had fixed his eyes upon a distorted fir-tree, planted by some former tenant in a tub that had once been green, and left there, years before, to rot away piecemeal.... At length, his eyes wandered to a little dirty window on the left, through which the face of the clerk was dimly visible; that worthy chancing to look up, he beckoned him to attend.

It is delightful, detail by detail, and we can stay with it because we feel, with the writer, that it hasn't been done before. This also means that it can't be done with the same effect again. It will lose its air of discovery, which is its virtue. Writing has always to be new; every talent is always burning itself out. Twenty-one years later, in *A Tale of Two Cities* (1859), in the wine-cask scene, the Dickensian hard stare has become technique, impressive but rhetorical, the detail oddly manufactured, the product more of mind and habit than of eye.

A large cask of wine had been dropped and broken ... and it lay on the stones just outside the door of the wine-shop, shattered like a walnut shell.

All the people within reach had suspended their business, or their idleness, to run to the spot and drink the wine. The rough, irregular stones of the street, pointing every way, and designed, one might have thought, expressly to lame all living creatures that approached them, had dammed it into little pools; these were surrounded, each by its own jostling group or crowd, according to its size. Some men kneeled down, made scoops of their two hands joined, and sipped, or tried to help women, who bent over their shoulders to sip, before the wine had all run out between their fingers. Others, men and women dipped in the puddles with little mugs of mutilated earthenware, or even with handkerchiefs from women's heads, which were squeezed dry into infants' mouths.

Only the shattered walnut and the mutilated mug are like the younger Dickens. The other details will not create revolutionary Paris (of seventy years before); they are building up more into the symbolism of the political cartoon.

Literature is the sum of its discoveries. What is derivative can be impressive and intelligent. It can give pleasure and it will have its season, short or long. But we will always want to go back to the originators. What matters in the end in literature, what is always there, is the truly good. And—though played-out forms can throw up miraculous sports like *The Importance of Being Earnest* or *Decline and Fall*—what is good is always what is new, in both form and content. What is good forgets whatever models it might have had, and is unexpected; we have to catch it on the wing. Writing of this quality cannot be taught in a writing course.

Literature, like all living art, is always on the move. It is part of its life that its dominant form should constantly change. No literary form—the Shakespearean play, the epic poem, the Restoration comedy, the essay, the work of history—can continue for very long at the same pitch of inspiration. If every creative talent is always burning itself out, every literary form is always getting to the end of what it can do.

The new novel gave nineteenth-century Europe a certain kind of news. The late twentieth century, surfeited with news, culturally far more confused, threatening again to be as full of tribal or folk movement as during the centuries of the Roman empire, needs another kind of interpretation. But the novel, still (in spite of appearances) mimicking the programme of the nineteenth-century originators, still feeding off the vision they created, can subtly distort the unaccommodating new reality. As a form it is now commonplace enough, and limited enough, to be teachable. It encourages a multitude of little narcissisms, from near and far; they stand in for originality and give the form an illusion of life. It is a vanity of the age (and commercial promotion) that the novel continues to be literature's final and highest expression.

Here I have to go back to the beginning. It was out of the colonial small change of the great nineteenth-century achievement that—perhaps through a teacher or a friend—the desire to be a writer came to my father in the late 1920s. He did become a writer, though not in the way he wanted. He did good work; his stories gave our community a past that would otherwise have been lost. But there was a mismatch between the ambition, coming from outside, from another culture, and our community, which had no living literary tradition; and my father's hard-won stories have found very few readers among the people they were about.

He passed on the writing ambition to me; and I, growing up in another age, have managed to see that ambition through almost to the end. But I remember how hard it was for me as a child to read serious books; two spheres of darkness separated me from them. Nearly all my imaginative life was in the cinema. Everything there was far away, but at the same time everything in that curious operatic world was accessible. It was a truly universal art. I don't think I overstate when I say that without the Hollywood of the 1930s and 1940s I would have been spiritually quite destitute. That cannot be shut out of this account of reading and writing. And I have to wonder now whether the talent that once went into imaginative literature didn't in this century go into the first fifty years of the glorious cinema.

1998

PART ONE

East Indian

IT WAS ABOUT thirteen or fourteen years ago. In those days Air France used to run an Epicurean Service between London and Paris. The advertisements taunted me. Poverty makes for recklessness, and one idle day in the long summer vacation I booked. The following morning I went with nervous expectation to the Kensington air terminal. There was another Indian in the lounge. He was about fifty and very small, neat with homburg and gold-rimmed spectacles, and looking packaged in a three-piece suit. He was pure buttoned-up joy: he too was an Epicurean traveller.

"You are coming from——?"

I had met enough Indians from India to know that this was less a serious inquiry than a greeting, in a distant land, from one Indian to another.

"Trinidad," I said. "In the West Indies. And you?"

He ignored my question. "But you look Indian."

"I am."

"Red Indian?" He suppressed a nervous little giggle.

"East Indian. From the West Indies."

He looked offended and wandered off to the bookstall. From this distance he eyed me assessingly. In the end curiosity overcame misgiving. He sat next to me on the bus to the airport. He sat next to me in the plane.

"Your first trip to Paris?" he asked.

"Yes."

"My fourth. I am a newspaperman. America, the United States of America, have you been there?"

"I once spent twelve hours in New York."

"I have been to the United States of America three times. I also know the Dominion of Canada. I don't like this aeroplane. I don't like the way it is wibrating. What sort do you think it is? I'll ask the steward."

He pressed the buzzer. The steward didn't come.

"At first I thought it was a Dakota. Now I feel it is a Wiking."

The steward bustled past, dropping white disembarkation cards into laps. The Indian seized the steward's soiled white jacket.

"Steward, is this aircraft a Wiking?"

"No, sir. Not a Viking. It's a Languedoc, a French plane, sir."

"Languedoc. Of course. That is one thing journalism teaches you. Always get to the bottom of everything."

We filled in our disembarkation cards. The Indian studied my passport.

"Trinidad, Trinidad," he said, as though searching for a face or a name.

Before he could find anything the Epicurean meal began. The harassed steward pulled out trays from the back of seats, slapped down monogrammed glasses and liquor miniatures. It was a short flight, which perhaps he had already made more than once that day, and he behaved like a man with problems at the other end.

"Indian," the Indian said reprovingly, "and you are drinking?"

"I am drinking."

"At home," he said, sipping his aperitif, "I *never* drink."

The steward was back, with a clutch of half-bottles of champagne.

"Champagne!" the Indian cried, as though about to clap his tiny hands. "Champagne!"

Corks were popping all over the aircraft. The trays of food came.

I grabbed the steward's dirty jacket.

"I am sorry," I said. "I should have told them. But I don't eat meat."

Holding two trays in one hand, he said, "I am sorry, sir. There is nothing else. The meals are not prepared on the plane."

"But you must have an egg or some fish or something."

"We have some cheese."

"But this is an Epicurean Service. You can't just give me a piece of cheese."

"I am sorry, sir."

I drank champagne with my bread and cheese.

"So you are not eating?"

"I am not eating."

"I enwy you." The Indian was champing through meats of various colours, sipping champagne and crying out for more. "I enwy you your wegetarianism. At home I am *strict* wegetarian. No one has even boiled an egg in my house."

The steward took away the remains of my bread and cheese, and gave me coffee, brandy, and a choice of liqueurs.

The Indian experimented swiftly. He sipped, he gulped. The flight was drawing to a close; we were already fastening our seat belts. His eyes were red and watery behind his spectacles. He stuck his hat on at comic angles and made faces at me. He nudged me in the ribs and cuffed me on the shoulder and giggled. He chucked me under the chin and sang: *"Wege-wege-wegetarian! Hin-du wege-tar-ian!"*

He was in some distress when we landed. His hat was still at a comic angle, but his flushed little face had a bottled-up solemnity. He was in for a hard afternoon. Even so, he composed himself for a farewell speech.

"My dear sir, I am a journalist and I have travelled. I hope you will permit me to say how much I appreciate it that, although separated by many generations and many thousands of miles of sea and ocean from the Motherland, you still keep up the customs and traditions of our religion. I *do* appreciate it. Allow me to congratulate you."

I was hungry, and my head was heavy. "No, no, my dear sir. Allow me to congratulate you."

TO BE a colonial is to be a little ridiculous and unlikely, especially in the eyes of someone from the metropolitan country. All immigrants and their descendants are colonials of one sort or another, and between the colonial and what one might call the metropolitan there always exists a muted mutual distrust. In England the image of the American is fixed. In Spain, where imperial glory has been dead for so long, they still whisper to you, an impartial outsider, about the loudness of *americanos*— to them people from Argentina and Uruguay. In an Athens hotel you can distinguish the Greek Americans, *back for a holiday* (special words in the vocabulary of immigrants), from the natives. The visitors speak with loud, exaggerated American accents, occasionally slightly flawed; the stances of the women are daring and self-conscious. The natives, overdoing the quiet culture and feminine modesty, appear to cringe with offence.

Yet to be Latin American or Greek American is to be known, to be a type, and therefore in some way to be established. To be an Indian or East Indian from the West Indies is to be a perpetual surprise to people outside the region. When you think of the West Indies you think of Columbus and the Spanish galleons, slavery and the naval rivalries of the eighteenth century. You might, more probably, think of calypsos and the Trinidad carnival and expensive sun and sand. When you think of the East you think of the Taj Mahal at the end of a cypress-lined vista and you think of holy men. You don't go to Trinidad, then, expecting to find Hindu pundits scuttling about country roads on motor-cycles; to see pennants with ancient devices fluttering from temples; to see mosques cool and white and rhetorical against the usual Caribbean buildings of concrete and corrugated iron; to find India celebrated in the street names of one whole district of Port of Spain; to see the Hindu festival of lights or the Muslim mourning ceremony for Husein, the Prophet's descendant, killed at the Battle of Kerbela in Arabia thirteen hundred years ago.

To be an Indian from Trinidad is to be unlikely. It is, in addition to everything else, to be the embodiment of an old verbal ambiguity. For this word "Indian" has been abused as no other word in the language; almost every time it is used it has to be qualified. There was a time in Europe when everything Oriental or everything a little unusual was judged to come from Turkey or India. So Indian ink is really Chinese ink and India paper first came from China. When in 1492 Columbus landed on the island of Guanahani he thought he had got to Cathay. He ought therefore to have called the people Chinese. But East was East. He called them Indians, and Indians they remained, walking Indian file through the Indian corn. And so, too, that American bird which to English-speaking people is the turkey is to the French *le dindon*, the bird of India.

so long as the real Indians remained on the other side of the world, there was little confusion. But when in 1845 these Indians began coming over to some of the islands Columbus had called the Indies, confusion became total. Slavery had been abolished in the British islands; the negroes refused to work for a master, and many plantations were faced with ruin. Indentured labourers were brought in from China, Portugal and India. The Indians fitted. More and more came. They were good agriculturalists and were encouraged to settle after their indentures had expired. Instead of a passage home they could take land. Many did. The indenture system lasted, with breaks, from 1845 until 1917, and in Trinidad alone the descendants of those immigrants who stayed number over a quarter of a million.

But what were these immigrants to be called? Their name had been appropriated three hundred and fifty years before. "Hindu" was a useful word, but it had religious connotations and would have offended the many Muslims among the immigrants. In the British territories the immigrants were called East Indians. In this way they were distinguished from the two other types of Indians in the islands: the American Indians and the West Indians. After a generation or two, the East Indians were regarded as settled inhabitants of the West Indies and were thought of as West Indian East Indians. Then a national feeling grew up. There was a cry for integration, and the West Indian East Indians became East Indian West Indians.

This didn't suit the Dutch. They had a colony called Surinam, or Dutch Guiana, on the north coast of South America. They also owned a good deal of the East Indies, and to them an East Indian was someone who came from the East Indies and was of Malay stock. (When you go to an Indian restaurant in Holland you don't go to an Indian restaurant; you go to an East Indian or Javanese restaurant.) In Surinam there were many genuine East Indians from the East Indies. So another name had to be found for the Indians from India who came to Surinam. The Dutch called them British Indians. Then, with the Indian nationalist agitation in India, the British Indians began to resent being called British Indians. The Dutch compromised by calling them Hindustanis.

East Indians, British Indians, Hindustanis. But the West Indies are part of the New World and these Indians of Trinidad are no longer of Asia. The temples and mosques exist and appear genuine. But the languages that came with them have decayed. The rituals have altered. Since open-air cremation is forbidden by the health authorities, Hindus are buried, not cremated. Their ashes are not taken down holy rivers into the ocean to become again part of the Absolute. There is no Ganges at hand, only a muddy stream called the Caroni. And the water that the Hindu priest sprinkles with a mango leaf around the sacrificial fire is not Ganges water but simple tap water. The holy city of Benares is far away, but the young Hindu at his initiation ceremony in Port of Spain will still take up his staff and beggar's bowl and say that he is off to Benares to study. His relatives will plead with him, and in the end he will lay down his staff, and there will be a ritual expression of relief.*

IT IS the play of a people who have been cut off. To be an Indian from Trinidad, then, is to be unlikely and exotic. It is also to be a little fraudulent. But so all immigrants become. In India itself there is the energetic community of Parsis. They fled from Persia to escape Muslim religious persecution. But over the years the very religion which they sought to preserve has become a matter of forms and especially of burial forms: in Bombay their dead are taken to the frighteningly named Towers of Silence and there exposed to vultures. They have adopted the language of the sheltering country and their own language has become a secret gibberish. Immigrants are people on their own. They cannot be judged by the standards of their older culture. Culture is like language, ever developing. There is no right and wrong, no purity from which there is decline. Usage sanctions everything.

And these Indians from Trinidad, despite their temples and rituals, so startling to the visitors, belong to the New World. They are immigrants; they have the drive and restlessness of immigrants. To them India is a word. In moments of self-distrust this word might suggest the Taj Mahal and an ancient civilization. But more usually it suggests other words, fearfully visualized, "famine," "teeming millions." And to many, India is no more than the memory of a depressed rural existence that survived in Trinidad until only the other day. Occasionally in the

---

*Cremation is now permitted; ashes are scattered in the Caroni; and Ganges water is now imported.

interior of the island a village of thatched roofs and mud-and-bamboo walls still recalls Bengal.

IN BENGAL lay the great port of Calcutta. There, from the vast depressed hinterland of eastern India, the emigrants assembled for the journey by sail, often lasting four months, to the West Indies. The majority came from the provinces of Bihar and eastern Uttar Pradesh; and even today—although heavy industry has come to Bihar—these areas are known for their poverty and backwardness. It is a dismal, dusty land, made sadder by ruins and place names that speak of ancient glory. For here was the land of the Buddha; here are the cities mentioned in the Hindu epics of three thousand years ago—like Ayodhya, from which my father's family came, today a ramshackle town of wholly contemporary squalor.

The land is flat, intolerably flat, with few trees to dramatize it. The forests to which reference is often made in the epics have disappeared. The winters are brief, and in the fierce summers the fields are white with dust. You are never out of sight of low mud-walled or brick-walled villages, and there are people everywhere. An impression of tininess in vastness: tiny houses, tiny poor fields, thin, stunted people, a land scratched into dust by an ever-growing population. It is a land of famine and apathy, and yet a land of rigid caste order. Everyone has his place. Effort is futile. His field is small, his time unlimited, but the peasant still scatters his seed broadcast. He lives from hand to mouth. The attitude is understandable. In this more than feudal society of India, everything once belonged to the king, and later to the landlord: it was unwise to be prosperous. A man is therefore defined and placed by his caste alone. To the peasant on this over-populated plain, all of India, all the world, has been narrowed to a plot of ground and a few relationships.

Travel is still not easy in those parts, and from there a hundred years ago the West Indies must have seemed like the end of the world. Yet so many left, taking everything—beds, brass vessels, musical instruments, images, holy books, sandalwood sticks, astrological almanacs. It was less an uprooting than it appears. They were taking India with them. With their blinkered view of the world they were able to re-create eastern Uttar Pradesh or Bihar wherever they went. They had been able to ignore the vastness of India; so now they ignored the strangeness in which they had been set. To leave India's sacred soil, to cross the "black water," was considered an act of self-defilement. So completely did these migrants re-create India in Trinidad that they imposed a similar restriction on those who wished to leave Trinidad.

In a more energetic society they would have been lost. But Trinidad was stagnant in the nineteenth century. The Indians endured and prospered. The India they re-created was allowed to survive. It was an India in which a revolution had occurred. It was an India in isolation, unsupported; an India without caste or the overwhelming pressures towards caste. Effort had a meaning, and soon India could be seen to be no more than a habit, a self-imposed psychological restraint, wearing thinner with the years. At the first blast from the New World—the Second World War, the coming of Americans to the islands—India fell away, and a new people seemed all at once to have been created. The colonial, of whatever society, is a product of revolution; and the revolution takes place in the mind.

Certain things remain: the temples, the food, the rites, the names, though these become steadily more Anglicised and less recognizable to Indians; or it might be a distaste for meat, derived from a Hindu background and surviving even an Epicurean flight between London and Paris. Certainly it was odd, when I was in India two years ago, to find that often, listening to a language I thought I had forgotten, I was understanding. Just a word or two, but they seemed to recall a past life and fleetingly they gave that sensation of an experience that has been lived before. But fleetingly, since for the colonial there can be no true return.

IN A DELHI club I met an Indian from Trinidad. I had last seen him fifteen years before. He was an adventurer. Now he was a little sad. He was an exile in the Motherland, and fifteen years had definitely taken him past youth; for him there were to be no more adventures. He was quiet and subdued. Then a worried, inquiring look came into his eyes.

"Tell me. I think we are way ahead of this bunch, don't you think?"

"But there's no question," I said.

He brightened; he looked relieved. He smiled; he laughed.

"I'm *so* glad you think so. It's what I *always* tell them. Come, have a drink."

We drank. We became loud, colonials together.

1965

Jasmine

ONE DAY about ten years ago, when I was editing a weekly literary programme for the BBC's Caribbean Service, a man from Trinidad came to see me in one of the freelances' rooms in the old Langham Hotel. He sat on the edge of the table, slapped down some sheets of typescript and said, "My name is Smith. I write about sex. I am also a nationalist." The sex was tepid, Maugham and coconut-water; but the nationalism was aggressive. Women swayed like coconut trees; their skins were the colour of the sapodilla, the inside of their mouths the colour of a cut star-apple; their teeth were as white as coconut kernels; and when they made love they groaned like bamboos in high wind.

The writer was protesting against what the English language had imposed on us. The language was ours, to use as we pleased. The literature that came with it was therefore of peculiar authority; but this literature was like an alien mythology. There was, for instance, Wordsworth's notorious poem about the daffodil. A pretty little flower, no doubt; but we had never seen it. Could the poem have any meaning for us? The superficial prompting of this argument, which would have confined all literatures to the countries of their origin, was political; but it was really an expression of dissatisfaction at the emptiness of our own formless, unmade society. To us, without a mythology,

45

all literatures were foreign. Trinidad was small, remote and unimportant, and we knew we could not hope to read in books of the life we saw about us. Books came from afar; they could offer only fantasy.

To open a book was to make an instant adjustment. Like the medieval sculptor of the North interpreting the Old Testament stories in terms of the life he knew, I needed to be able to adapt. All Dickens's descriptions of London I rejected; and though I might retain Mr. Micawber and the others in the clothes the illustrator gave them, I gave them the faces and voices of people I knew and set them in buildings and streets I knew. The process of adaptation was automatic and continuous. Dickens's rain and drizzle I turned into tropical downpours; the snow and fog I accepted as conventions of books. Anything—like an illustration—which embarrassed me by proving how weird my own reaction was, anything which sought to remove the characters from the made-up world in which I set them, I rejected.

I went to books for fantasy; at the same time I required reality. The gypsies of *The Mill on the Floss* were a fabrication and a disappointment, discrediting so much that was real: to me gypsies were mythical creatures who belonged to the pure fantasy of Hans Christian Andersen and *The Heroes*. Disappointing, too, was the episode of the old soldier's sword, because I thought that swords belonged to ancient times; and the Tom Tulliver I had created walked down the street where I lived. The early parts of *The Mill on the Floss*, then; chapters of *Oliver Twist*, *Nicholas Nickleby*, *David Copperfield;* some of the novels of H. G. Wells; a short story by Conrad called "The Lagoon": all these which in the beginning I read or had read to me I set in Trinidad, accepting, rejecting, adapting and peopling in my own way. I never read to find out about foreign countries. Everything in books was foreign; everything had to be subjected to adaptation; and everything in, say, an English novel which worked and was of value to me at once ceased to be specifically English. Mr. Murdstone worked; Mr. Pickwick and his club didn't. *Jane Eyre* and *Wuthering Heights* worked; *Pride and Prejudice* didn't. Maupassant worked; Balzac didn't.

I went to books for a special sort of participation. The only social division I accepted was that between rich and poor, and any society more elaborately ordered seemed insubstantial and alien. In literature such a society was more than alien; it was excluding, it made nonsense of my fantasies and more and more, as I grew older and thought of writing myself, it made me despairingly conscious of the poverty and haphazardness of my own society. I might adapt Dickens to Trinidad; but it seemed impossible that the life I knew in Trinidad could ever be turned into a book. If landscapes do not start to be real until they have been interpreted by an artist, so, until they have been written about, societies appear to be without shape and *embarrassing*. It was embarrassing to be reminded by a Dickens illustration of the absurdity of my adaptations; it was equally embarrassing to attempt to write of what I saw. Very little of what I read was of help. It would have been possible to assume the sensibility of a particular writer. But no writer, however individual his vision, could be separated from this society. The vision was alien; it diminished my own and did not give me the courage to do a simple thing like mentioning the name of a Port of Spain street.

Fiction or any work of the imagination, whatever its quality, hallows its subject. To attempt, with a full consciousness of established authoritative mythologies, to give a quality of myth to what was agreed to be petty and ridiculous—Frederick Street in Port of Spain, Marine Square, the districts of Laventille and Barataria—to attempt to use these names required courage. It was, in a way, the rejection of the familiar, meaningless word— the rejection of the unknown daffodil to put it no higher—and was as self-conscious as the attempt to have sapodilla-skinned women groaning like bamboos in high wind.

．．．．．

WITH ALL English literature accessible, then, my position was like that of the maharaja in *Hindoo Holiday*, who, when told by the Christian lady that God was here, there and everywhere, replied, "But what use is that to *me*?" Something of more pertinent virtue was needed, and this was provided by some local short stories. These stories, perhaps a dozen in all, never published outside Trinidad, converted what I saw into "writing." It was through them that I began to appreciate the distorting, distilling power of the writer's art. Where I had seen a drab haphazardness they found order; where I would have attempted to romanticize, to render my subject equal with what I had read, they accepted. They provided a starting-point for further observation; they did not trigger off fantasy. Every writer is, in the long run, on his own; but it helps, in the most practical way, to have a tradition. The English language was mine; the tradition was not.

Literature, then, was mainly fantasy. Perhaps it was for this reason that, although I had at an early age decided to be a writer and at the age of eighteen had left Trinidad with that ambition, I did not start writing seriously until I was nearly twenty-three. My material had not been sufficiently hallowed by a tradition; I was not fully convinced of its importance; and some embarrassment remained. My taste for literature had developed into a love of language, the word in isolation. At school my subjects were French and Spanish; and the pleasures of the language were at least as great as those of the literature. Maupassant and Molière were rich; but it was more agreeable to spend an hour with the big Harrap French-English dictionary, learning more of the language through examples, than with Corneille or Racine. And it was because I thought I had had enough of these languages (both now grown rusty) that when I came to England to go to university I decided to read English.

This was a mistake. The English course had little to do with literature. It was a "discipline" seemingly aimed at juvenile antiquarians. It by-passed the novel and the prose "asides" in which so much of the richness of the literature lay. By a common and curious consent it concentrated on poetry; and since it stopped at the eighteenth century it degenerated, after an intensive study of Shakespeare, into a lightning survey of minor and often severely local talents. I had looked forward to wandering among large tracts of writing; I was presented with "texts." The metaphysicals were a perfect subject for study, a perfect part of a discipline; but, really, they had no value for me. Dryden, for all the sweet facility of his prose, was shallow and dishonest; did his "criticism" deserve such reverential attention? *Gulliver's Travels* was excellent; but could *The Tale of a Tub* and *The Battle of the Books* be endured?

The fact was, I had no taste for scholarship, for tracing the growth of schools and trends. I sought continuously to relate literature to life. My training at school didn't help. We had few libraries, few histories of literature to turn to; and when we wrote essays on *Tartuffe* we wrote out of a direct response to the play. Now I discovered that the study of literature had been made scientific, that each writer had to be approached through the booby-traps of scholarship. There were the bound volumes of the Publications of the Modern Language Association of America, affectionately referred to by old and knowing young as PMLA. The pages that told of Chaucer's knowledge of astronomy or astrology (the question came up every year) were black and bloated and furred with handling, and even some of the pencilled annotations (*No, Norah!*) had grown faint. I developed a physical distaste for these bound volumes and the libraries that housed them.

Delight cannot be taught and measured; scholarship can; and my reaction was irrational. But it seemed to me scholarship of such a potted order. A literature was not being explored; it had been codified and reduced to a few pages of "text," some volumes of "background" and more of "criticism"; and to this mixture a mathematical intelligence might have been applied. There were discoveries, of course: Shakespeare, Marlowe, Restoration comedy. But my distaste for the study of literature led to a sense of being more removed than ever from the literature itself.

The language remained mine, and it was to the study of its development that I turned with pleasure. Here was enough to satisfy my love of language; here was unexpected adventure. It might not have been easy to see Chaucer as a great imaginative writer or to find in the *Prologue* more than a limited piece of observation which had been exceeded a thousand times; but Chaucer as a handler of a new, developing language was exciting. And my pleasure in Shakespeare was doubled. In Trinidad English writing had been for me a starting-point for fantasy. Now, after some time in England, it was possible to isolate the word, to separate the literature from the language.

Language can be so deceptive. It has taken me much time to realize how bad I am at interpreting the conventions and modes of English speech. This speech has never been better dissected than in the early stories of Angus Wilson. This is the judgement of today; my first responses to these stories were as blundering and imperfect as the responses of Professor Pforzheim to the stern courtesies of his English colleagues in *Anglo-Saxon Attitudes*. But while knowledge of England has made English writing more truly accessible, it has made participation more difficult; it has made impossible the exercise of fantasy, the reader's complementary response. I am inspecting an alien society, which I yet know, and I am looking for particular social comment. And to re-read now the books which lent themselves to fantastic interpretation in Trinidad is to see, almost with dismay, how English they are. The illustrations to Dickens cannot now be dismissed. And so, with knowledge, the books have ceased to be mine.

IT IS the English literary vice, this looking for social comment; and it is difficult to resist. The preoccupation of the novelists reflects a society ruled by convention and manners in the fullest sense, an ordered society of the self-aware who read not so much for adventure as to compare, to find what they know or think they know. A writer is to be judged by what he reports on; the working-class writer is a working-class writer and no more. So writing develops into the private language of a particular society. There are new reports, new discoveries: they are rapidly absorbed. And with each discovery the society's image of itself becomes more fixed and the society looks further inward. It has too many points of reference; it has been written about too often; it has read too much. Angus Wilson's characters, for instance, are great readers; they are steeped in Dickens and Jane Austen. Soon there will be characters steeped in Angus Wilson; the process is endless. Sensibility will overlie sensibility: the grossness of experience will be refined away by self-awareness. Writing will become Arthur Miller's definition of a newspaper: a nation talking to itself. And even those who have the key will be able only to witness, not to participate.

All literatures are regional; perhaps it is only the placelessness of a Shakespeare or the blunt communication of "gross" experience as in Dickens that makes them appear less so. Or perhaps it is a lack of knowledge in the reader. Even in this period of "internationalism" in letters we have seen literatures turning more and more inward, developing languages that are more and more private. Perhaps in the end literature will write itself out, and all its pleasures will be those of the word.

A LITTLE over three years ago I was in British Guiana. I was taken late one afternoon to meet an elderly lady of a distinguished Christian Indian family. Our political attitudes were too opposed to make any discussion of the current crisis profitable. We talked of the objects in her verandah and of the old days. Suddenly the tropical daylight was gone, and from the garden came the scent of a flower. I knew the flower from my childhood; yet I had never found out its name. I asked now.

"We call it jasmine."

Jasmine! So I had known it all those years! To me it had been a word in a book, a word to play with, something removed from the dull vegetation I knew.

The old lady cut a sprig for me. I stuck it in the top button-hole of my open shirt. I smelled it as I walked back to the hotel. Jasmine, jasmine. But the word and the flower had been separate in my mind for too long. They did not come together.

1964

Prologue to an Autobiography

1

IT IS NOW nearly thirty years since, in a BBC room in London, on an old BBC typewriter, and on smooth, "non-rustle" BBC script paper, I wrote the first sentence of my first publishable book. I was some three months short of my twenty-third birthday. I had left Oxford ten months before, and was living in London, trying to keep afloat and, in between, hoping to alleviate my anxiety but always only adding to it, trying to get started as a writer.

At Oxford I had been supported by a Trinidad government scholarship. In London I was on my own. The only money I got—eight guineas a week, less "deductions"—came from the BBC Caribbean Service. My only piece of luck in the past year, and even in the past two years, had been to get a part-time job editing and presenting a weekly literary programme for the Caribbean.

The Caribbean Service was on the second floor of what had been the Langham Hotel, opposite Broadcasting House. On this floor the BBC had set aside a room for people like me, "free-lances"—to me then not a word suggesting freedom and valour, but suggesting only people on the fringe of a mighty enterprise, a depressed and suppliant class: I would have given a lot to be "staff."

The freelances' room didn't encourage thoughts of radio glory; it was strictly for the production of little scripts. Something of the hotel atmosphere remained: in the great Victorian-Edwardian days of the Langham Hotel (it was mentioned in at least one Sherlock Holmes story), the freelances' room might have been a pantry. It was at the back of the heavy brick building, and gloomy when the ceiling lights were turned off. It wasn't cheerful when the lights were on: ochre walls with a peagreen dado, the gloss paint tarnished; a radiator below the window, with grit on the sill; two or three chairs, a telephone, two tables and two old standard typewriters.

It was in that Victorian-Edwardian gloom, and at one of those typewriters, that late one afternoon, without having any idea where I was going, and not perhaps intending to type to the end of the page, I wrote: *Every morning when he got up Hat would sit on the banister of his back verandah and shout across, "What happening there, Bogart?"*

That was a Port of Spain memory. It seemed to come from far back, but it was only eleven or twelve years old. It came from the time when we—various branches of my mother's family—were living in Port of Spain, in a house that belonged to my mother's mother. We were country people, Indians, culturally still Hindus; and this move to Port of Spain was in the nature of a migration: from the Hindu and Indian countryside to the white-negro-mulatto town.

Hat was our neighbor on the street. He wasn't negro or mulatto. But we thought of him as half-way there. He was a Port of Spain Indian. The Port of Spain Indians—there were pockets of them—had no country roots, were individuals, hardly a community, and were separate from us for an additional reason: many of them were Madrassis, descendants of South Indians, not Hindi-speaking, and not people of caste. We didn't see in them any of our own formalities or restrictions; and though we lived raggedly ourselves (and were far too numerous for the house), we thought of the other Indians in the street only as street people.

That shout of "Bogart!" was in more than one way a shout from the street. And, to add to the incongruity, it was addressed to someone in our yard: a young man, very quiet, yet another person connected in some way with my mother's family. He had come not long before from the country and was living in the separate one-room building at the back of our yard.

We called this room the "servant room." Port of Spain houses, up to the 1930s, were built with these separate servant rooms—verandah-less little boxes, probably descended in style from the ancillary "negro-houses" of slave times. I suppose that in one or two houses in our street servants of the house actually lived in the servant room. But generally it wasn't so. Servant rooms, because of the privacy they offered, were in demand, and not by servants.

It was wartime. The migration of my own family into the town had become part of a more general movement. People of all conditions were coming into Port of Spain to work at the two American bases. One of those bases had been built on recently reclaimed land just at the end of our street—eight houses down. Twice a day we heard the bugles; Americans, formal in their uniforms, with their khaki ties tucked into their shirts, were another part of the life of our street. The street was busy; the yards were crowded. Our yard was more crowded than most. No servant ever lodged in our servant room. Instead, the room sheltered a succession of favoured transients, on their way to better things. Before the big family rush, some of these transients had been outsiders; but now they were mostly relations or people close to the family, like Bogart.

The connection of Bogart with my mother's family was unusual. At the turn of the century Bogart's father and my mother's father had travelled out together from India as indentured immigrants. At some time during the long and frightening journey they had sworn a bond of brotherhood; that was the bond that was being honoured by their descendants.

Bogart's people were from the Punjab, and handsome. The two brothers we had got to know were ambitious men, rising in white-collar jobs. One was a teacher; the other (who had passed through the servant room) was a weekend sportsman who, in the cricket season, regularly got his name in the paper. Bogart didn't have the education or the ambition of his brothers; it wasn't clear what he did for a living. He was placid, without any pronounced character, detached, and in that crowded yard oddly solitary.

Once he went away. When he came back, some weeks or months later, it was said that he had been "working on a ship." Port of Spain was a colonial port, and we thought of sailors as very rough, the dregs. So this business of working on a ship—though it suggested money as well as luck, for the jobs were not easy to come by—also held suggestions of danger. It was something for the reckless and the bohemian. But it must have suited Bogart, because after a time he went away—disappeared—again.

There was a story this time that he had gone to Venezuela. He came back; but I had no memory of his return. His adventures—if he had had any—remained unknown to me. I believe I was told that the first time he had gone away, to work on the ship, he had worked as a cook. But that might have been a story I made up myself. All that I knew of Bogart while he lived in the servant room was what, as a child, I saw from a distance. He and his comings and goings were part of the confusion and haphazardness and crowd of that time.

I saw a little more of him four or five years later. The war was over. The American base at the end of the street was closed. The buildings were pulled down, and the local contractor, who knew someone in our family, gave us the run of the place for a few days, to pick up what timber we wanted. My mother's extended family was breaking up into its component parts; we were all leaving my grandmother's house. My father had bought a house of his own; I used timber from the old American base to make a new front gate. Soon I had got the Trinidad government scholarship that was to take me to Oxford.

Bogart was still reportedly a traveller. And in Trinidad now he was able to do what perhaps he had always wanted to do: to put as much distance as possible between himself and people close to him. He was living in Carenage, a seaside village five miles or so west of Port of Spain. Carenage was a negro-mulatto place, with a Spanish flavour (*'pagnol*, in the local French patois). There were few Indians in Carenage; that would have suited Bogart.

With nothing to do, waiting to go away, I was restless, and I sometimes cycled out to Carenage. It was pleasant after the hot ride to splash about in the rocky sea, and pleasant after that to go and have a Coca-Cola at Bogart's. He lived in a side street, a wandering lane, with yards that were half bush, half built-up. He was a tailor now, apparently with customers; and he sat at his machine in his open shop, welcoming but undemonstrative, as placid, as without conversation, and as solitary as ever. But he was willing to play with me. He was happy to let me paint a sign-board for his shop. The idea was mine, and he took it seriously. He had a carpenter build a board of new wood; and on this, over some days, after priming and painting, I did the sign. He put it up over his shop door, and I thought it looked genuine, a real sign. I was amazed; it was the first sign-board I had ever done.

The time then came for me to go to England. I left Bogart in Carenage. And that was where he had continued to live in my memory, faintly, never a figure in the foreground: the man who had worked on a ship, then gone to Venezuela, sitting placidly ever after at his sewing machine, below my sign, in his little concrete house-and-shop.

That was Bogart's story, as I knew it. And—after all our migrations within Trinidad, after my own trip to England and my time at Oxford—that was all the story I had in mind when—after two failed attempts at novels—I sat at the type-writer in the freelances' room in the Langham Hotel, to try once more to be a writer. And luck was with me that afternoon. *Every morning when he got up Hat would sit on the banister of his back verandah and shout across, "What happening there, Bogart?"* Luck was with me, because that first sentence was so direct, so unclut-tered, so without complications, that it provoked the sentence that was to follow. *Bogart would turn in his bed and mumble softly, so that no one heard, "What happening there, Hat?"*

The first sentence was true. The second was invention. But together—to me, the writer—they had done something extraor-dinary. Though they had left out everything—the setting, the historical time, the racial and social complexities of the people concerned—they had suggested it all; they had created the world of the street. And together, as sentences, words, they had set up a rhythm, a speed, which dictated all that was to follow.

The story developed a first-person narrator. And for the sake of speed, to avoid complications, to match the rhythm of what had gone before, this narrator could not be myself. My narrator lived alone with his mother in a house on the street. He had no father; he had no other family. So, very simply, all the crowd of my mother's extended family, as cumbersome in real life as it would have been to a writer, was abolished; and, again out of my wish to simplify, I had a narrator more in tune with the life of the street than I had been.

Bogart's tailoring business, with the sign-board I had done for him, I transferred from the Carenage side street to the Port of Spain servant room, and with it there came some hint of the silent companionableness I had found in Bogart at that later period. The servant room and the street—the houses, the pave-ments, the open yards, the American base at the end of the street—became like a stage set. Anyone might walk down the street; anyone might turn up in the servant room. It was enough—given the rhythm of the narrative and its accumulating suggestions of street life—for the narrator to say so. So Bogart could come and go, without fuss. When, in the story, he left the servant room for the first time, it took little—just the dropping of a few names—to establish the idea of the street as a kind of club.

So that afternoon in the Langham Hotel Port of Spain memories, disregarded until then, were simplified and transformed. The speed of the narrative—that was the speed of the writer. And everything that was later to look like considered literary devices came only from the anxiety of the writer. I wanted above all to take the story to the end. I feared that if I stopped too long anywhere I might lose faith in what I was doing, give up once more and be left with nothing.

Speed dictated the solution of the mystery of Bogart. He wished to be free (of Hindu family conventions, but this wasn't stated in the story). He was without ambition, and had no skill; in spite of the sign-board, he was hardly a tailor. He was an unremarkable man, a man from the country, to whom mystery and the name of Bogart had been given by the street, which had its own city sense of drama. If Bogart spent whole afternoons in his servant room playing Patience, it was because he had no other way of passing the time. If, until he fell into the character of the film Bogart, he had no conversation, it was because he had little to say. The street saw him as sensual, lazy, cool. He was in fact passive. The emotional entanglements that called him away from the street were less than heroic. With women, Bogart—unlike most men of the street—had taken the easy way out. He was that flabby, emasculated thing, a bigamist. So, looking only for freedom, the Bogart of my story had ended up as a man on the run. It was only in the solitude of his servant room that he could be himself, at peace. It was only with the men and boys of the street that he could be a man.

The story was short, three thousand words, two foolscap sheets and a bit. I had—a conscious piece of magic that afternoon—set the typewriter at single space, to get as much as possible on the first sheet and also to create the effect of the printed page.

People were in and out of the freelances' room while I typed. Some would have dropped by at the BBC that afternoon for the company and the chat, and the off-chance of a commission by a producer for some little script. Some would have had work to do.

I suppose Ernest Eytle would have come in, to sit at the other typewriter and to peck, with many pauses, at the "links" or even a "piece" for the magazine programme. And Ernest's beautifully spoken words, crackling over the short wave that evening, would suggest a busy, alert man, deep in the metropolitan excitements of London, sparing a few minutes for his radio talk. He was a mulatto from British Guiana. He was dark-suited, fat and slow; when, some years later, I heard he had died, I was able mentally to transfer him, without any change, and without any feeling of shock, to a coffin. As much as broadcasting, Ernest liked the pub life around Broadcasting House. This sitting at the typewriter in the gloomy freelances' room was like an imposition; and Ernest, whenever he paused to think, would rub a heavy hand down his forehead to his eyebrows, which he pushed back the wrong way; and then, like a man brushing away cobwebs, he would appear to dust his cheek, his nose, his lips and chin.

Having done that with Ernest, I should say that my own typing posture in those days was unusual. My shoulders were thrown back as far as they could go; my spine was arched. My knees were drawn right up; my shoes rested on the topmost struts of the chair, left side and right side. So, with my legs wide apart, I sat at the typewriter with something like a monkey crouch.

THE FREELANCES' room was like a club: chat, movement, the separate anxieties of young or youngish men below the passing fellowship of the room. That was the atmosphere I was writing in. That was the atmosphere I gave to Bogart's Port of Spain street. Partly for the sake of speed, and partly because my memory or imagination couldn't rise to it, I had given his servant room hardly any furniture: the Langham room itself was barely furnished. And I benefited from the fellowship of the room that afternoon. Without that fellowship, without the response of the three men who read the story, I might not have wanted to go on with what I had begun.

I passed the three typed sheets around.

John Stockbridge was English. He worked for many BBC programmes, domestic and overseas. Unlike the rest of us, he carried a briefcase; and that briefcase suggested method, steadiness, many commissions. At our first meeting in the freelances' room three or four months before, he hadn't been too friendly—he no doubt saw me as an Oxford man, untrained, stepping just like that into regular radio work, taking the bread out of the mouths of more experienced men. But then his attitude towards me had become one of schoolmasterly concern. He wanted to rescue me from what, with his English eyes, he saw as my self-neglect. He wanted me to make a better job of myself, to present myself well, to wear better clothes, and especially to get rid of my dingy working-class overcoat. (I knew nothing about clothes, but I had always thought the overcoat was wrong: it had been chosen for me, before I went up to Oxford, by the Maltese manageress of an Earl's Court boarding house.) Now, after he had read the story, John made a serious face and spoke a prodigious prophecy about my future as a writer. On such little evidence! But it was his way of finally accepting my ambition and my London life, and giving me a little blessing.

Andrew Salkey was a Jamaican. He worked in a nightclub, was also trying to get started as a writer, and had just begun to do broadcasts, talks and readings. He compared learning to write with trying to wrap a whip around a rail; he thought I had begun to make the whip "stick." He detected, and made me take out, one or two early sentences where I had begun to lose faith in the material and had begun to ridicule, not the characters, but the idea that what I was doing was a real story.

The most wholehearted acceptance came from Gordon Woolford. He was from British Guiana. He came from a distinguished colonial family. He said he had some African ancestry, but it didn't show. Some deep trouble with his father had kept Gordon away from his family and committed him, after a privileged pre-war upbringing in Belgium and England, to a hard bohemian life in London. He was an unusually handsome man, in his mid-thirties. He had married a French girl, whom he had met when she was an assistant in one of the big London stores. That marriage had just broken up. Gordon was writing a novel about it, *On the Rocks;* it wasn't something he was going to finish. He changed jobs often; he loved writing; his favourite book—at least it was always with him during his drinking bouts—was *Scoop.*

Something in the Bogart story touched Gordon. When he finished reading the story he folded the sheets carefully; with a gesture as of acceptance he put the sheets in his inner jacket pocket; and then he led me out to the BBC club—he was not on the wagon that day. He read the story over again, and he made me read it with him, line by line, assessing the words and the tone: we might have been rehearsing a broadcast. The manuscript still has his foldmarks and his wine stains.

During the writing of the Bogart story some memory—very vague, as if from a forgotten film—had come to me of the man who in 1938 or 1939, five years before Bogart, had lived in his servant room. He was a negro carpenter; the small sheltered space between the servant room and the back fence was at once his kitchen and workshop. I asked him one day what he was making. He said—wonderfully to the six-year-old child who had asked the question—that he was making "the thing without a name."

It was the carpenter's story that I settled down to write the next day in the freelances' room. I had little to go on. But I had a street, already peopled; I had an atmosphere; and I had a narrator. I stuck to the magic of the previous day: the non-rustle BBC paper, the typewriter set at single space. And I was conscious, with Gordon Woolford's help, of certain things I had stumbled on the previous day: never to let the words get too much in the way, to be fast, to add one concrete detail to another, and above all to keep the tone right.

I mentally set the servant room in another yard. *The only thing that Popo, who called himself a carpenter, ever built was the little galvanized-iron workshop under the mango tree at the back of his yard.* And then scattered memories, my narrator, the life of the street, and my own childhood sense (as a six-year-old coming suddenly to Port of Spain from the Hindu rigours of my grandmother's house in the country) of the intensity of the pleasures of people on the street, gave the carpenter a story. He was an idler, a happy man, a relisher of life; but then his wife left him.

Over the next few days the street grew. Its complexities didn't need to be pointed; they simply became apparent. People who had only been names in one story got dialogue in the next, then became personalities; and old personalities became more familiar. Memory provided the material; city folklore as well, and city songs. An item from a London evening paper (about a postman throwing away his letters) was used. My narrator consumed material, and he seemed to be able to process every kind of material.

Even Gordon was written into the street. We were on the top of a bus one evening, going back from the BBC to Kilburn, the Irish working-class area where I lived in two rooms in the house of a BBC commissionaire. Gordon was talking of some early period of his life, some period of luxury and promise. Then he broke off, said, "But that was a long time ago," and looked down through the reflections of glass into the street. That went to my heart. Within a few days I was to run it into the memory of a negro ballad-maker, disturbed but very gentle, who had called at my grandmother's house in Port of Spain one day to sell copies of his poems, single printed sheets, and had told me a little of his life.

The stories became longer. They could no longer be written in a day. They were not always written in the freelances' room. The technique became more conscious; it was not always possible to write fast. Beginnings, and the rhythms they established, didn't always come naturally; they had to be worked for. And then the material, which at one time had seemed inexhaustible, dried up. I had come to the end of what I could do with the street, in that particular way. *My mother said, "You getting too wild in this place. I think is high time you leave."* My narrator left the street, as I had left Trinidad five years before. And the excitement I had lived with for five or six weeks was over.

I had written a book, and I felt it to be real. That had been my ambition for years, and an urgent ambition for the past year. And I suppose that if the book had had some response outside the freelances' room I might have been a little more secure in my talent, and my later approach to writing would have been calmer; it is just possible.

But I knew only anxiety. The publisher that Andrew Salkey took the book to sent no reply for three months (the book remained unpublished for four years). And—by now one long year out of Oxford—I was trying to write another, and discovering that to have written a book was not to be a writer. Looking for a new book, a new narrative, episodes, I found myself as uncertain, and as pretending to be a writer, as I had been before I had written the story of Bogart.

To be a writer, I thought, was to have the conviction that one could go on. I didn't have that conviction. And even when the new book had been written I didn't think of myself as a writer. I thought I should wait until I had written three. And when, a year after writing the second, I had written the third, I thought I should wait until I had written six. On official forms I described myself as a "broadcaster," thinking the word nondescript, suitable to someone from the freelances' room; until a BBC man, "staff," told me it was boastful.

So I became "writer." Though to myself an unassuageable anxiety still attached to the word, and I was still, for its sake, practising magic. I never bought paper to write on. I preferred to use "borrowed," non-rustle BBC paper; it seemed more casual, less likely to attract failure. I never numbered my pages, for fear of not getting to the end. (This drew the only comment Ernest Eytle made about my writing. Sitting idly at his typewriter one day in the freelances' room, he read some of my pages, apparently with goodwill. Then, weightily, he said, "I'll tell you what you should do with this." I waited. He said, "You should number the pages. In case they get mixed up.") And on the finished manuscripts of my first four books—half a million words—I never with my own hand typed or wrote my name. I always asked someone else to do that for me. Such anxiety; such ambition.

The ways of my fantasy, the process of creation, remained mysterious to me. For everything that was false or didn't work and had to be discarded, I felt that I alone was responsible. For everything that seemed right I felt I had only been a vessel. There was the recurring element of luck, or so it seemed to me. True, and saving, knowledge of my subject—beginning with Bogart's street—always seemed to come during the writing.

This element of luck isn't so mysterious to me now. As diarists and letter-writers repeatedly prove, any attempt at narrative can give value to an experience which might otherwise evaporate away. When I began to write about Bogart's street I began to sink into a tract of experience I hadn't before contemplated as a writer. This blindness might seem extraordinary in someone who wanted so much to be a writer. Half a writer's work, though, is the discovery of his subject. And a problem for me was that my life had been varied, full of upheavals and moves: from my grandmother's Hindu house in the country, still close to the rituals and social ways of village India; to Port of Spain, the negro and G.I. life of its streets, the other, ordered life of my colonial English school, which was called Queen's Royal College; and then Oxford, London and the free-lances' room at the BBC. Trying to make a beginning as a writer, I didn't know where to focus.

In England I was also a colonial. Out of the stresses of that, and out of my worship of the name of writer, I had without knowing it fallen into the error of thinking of writing as a kind of display. My very particularity—which was the subject sitting on my shoulder—had been encumbering me.

The English or French writer of my age had grown up in a world that was more or less explained. He wrote against a back-ground of knowledge. I couldn't be a writer in the same way, because to be a colonial, as I was, was to be spared knowledge. It was to live in an intellectually restricted world; it was to accept those restrictions. And the restrictions could become attractive.

Every morning when he got up Hat would sit on the banister of his back verandah and shout across, "What happening there, Bo-gart?" That was a good place to begin. But I couldn't stay there. My anxiety constantly to prove myself as a writer, the need to write another book and then another, led me away.

There was much in that call of "Bogart!" that had to be examined. It was spoken by a Port of Spain Indian, a descen-dant of nineteenth-century indentured immigrants from South India; and Bogart was linked in a special Hindu way with my mother's family. So there was a migration from India to be con-sidered, a migration within the British empire. There was my Hindu family, with its fading memories of India; there was India itself. And there was Trinidad, with its past of slavery, its mixed population, its racial antagonisms and its changing politi-cal life; once part of Venezuela and the Spanish empire, now English-speaking, with the American base and an open-air cinema at the end of Bogart's street. And just across the Gulf of Paria was Venezuela, the sixteenth-century land of El Dorado, now a country of dictators, but drawing Bogart out of his servant room with its promise of Spanish sexual adventure and the promise of a job in its oil fields.

And there was my own presence in England, writing: the career wasn't possible in Trinidad, a small, mainly agricultural colony: my vision of the world couldn't exclude that important fact.

So step by step, book by book, though seeking each time only to write another book, I eased myself into knowledge. To write was to learn. Beginning a book, I always felt I was in possession of all the facts about myself; at the end I was always surprised. The book before always turned out to have been written by a man with incomplete knowledge. And the very first, the one begun in the freelances' room, seemed to have been written by an innocent, a man at the beginning of knowledge about both himself and the writing career that had been his ambition from childhood.

2

THE AMBITION to be a writer was given me by my father. He was a journalist for much of his working life. This was an unusual occupation for a Trinidad Indian of his generation. My father was born in 1906. At that time the Indians of Trinidad were a separate community, mainly rural and Hindi-speaking, attached to the sugar estates of central and southern Trinidad. Many of the Indians of 1906 had been born in India and had come out to Trinidad as indentured labourers on five-year contracts. This form of Indian contract labour within the British empire ended, as a result of nationalist agitation in India, only in 1917.

In 1929 my father began contributing occasional articles on Indian topics to the *Trinidad Guardian*. In 1932, when I was born, he had become the *Guardian* staff correspondent in the little market town of Chaguanas. Chaguanas was in the heart of the sugar area and the Indian area of Trinidad. It was where my mother's family was established. Contract labour was far behind them; they were big landowners.

Two years or so after I was born my father left the *Guardian*, for reasons that were never clear to me. For some years he did odd jobs here and there, now attached to my mother's family, now going back to the protection of an uncle by marriage, a rich man, founder and part owner of the biggest bus company on the island. Poor himself, with close relations who were still agricultural labourers, my father dangled all his life in a half-dependence and half-esteem between these two powerful families.

In 1938 my father was taken on by the *Guardian* again, this time as a city reporter. And we—my father, my mother and their five children, our own little nucleus within my mother's extended family—moved to Port of Spain, to the house owned by my mother's mother. That was when I was introduced to the life of the street (and the mystery of the negro carpenter in the servant room, making "the thing without a name"). That was also when I got to know my father.

I had lived before then (at least in my own memory) in my mother's family house in Chaguanas. I knew I had a father, but I also knew and accepted that—like the fathers of others of my cousins—he was not present. There was a gift one year of a very small book of English poetry; there was a gift another time of a toy set of carpenter's tools. But the man himself remained vague.

He must have been in the house, though; because in the subsidiary two-storey wooden house at the back of the main building there were—on the inner wall of the upstairs verandah—jumbled ghostly impressions of banners or posters he had painted for someone in my mother's family who had fought a local election. The cotton banners had been stretched on the verandah wall; the beautiful oil paint, mainly red, had soaked through, disfiguring (or simply adding to) the flowered designs my mother's father (now dead) had had painted on the lower part of the verandah wall. The glory, of the election and my father's banners, belonged to the past; I accepted that.

My mother's family house in Chaguanas was a well-known local "big house." It was built in the North Indian style. It had balustraded roof terraces, and the main terrace was decorated at either end with a statue of a rampant lion. I didn't like or dislike living there; it was all I knew. But I liked the move to Port of Spain, to the emptier house, and the pleasures and sights of the city: the squares, the gardens, the children's playground, the streetlights, the ships in the harbour.

There was no American base at the end of the street. The land, still hardly with a name, known only as Docksite, had just been reclaimed, and the grey mud dredged up from the harbour was still drying out, making wonderful patterns as it crusted and cracked. After the shut-in compound life of the house in Chaguanas, I liked living on a city street. I liked looking at other people, other families. I liked the way things looked. In the morning the shadows of houses and trees fell on the pavement opposite; in the afternoon our pavement was in shadow. And I liked the municipal order of each day: the early-morning cleaning of the streets, with the hydrants turned on to flood the green-slimed gutters with fresh water; the later collection of refuse; the passing in mid-morning of the ice-cart.

Our house stood on high concrete pillars. The newspaper man threw the *Guardian* as high as he could up the concrete front steps. This delivery of a paper was one of the novelties of my Port of Spain life. And I also knew that, because my father worked for the *Guardian*, the paper was delivered free. So I had a feeling of privilege, a double sense of drama. And just as I had inherited or been given a feeling for lettering, so now I began to be given ambitions connected with the printed word. But these ambitions were twisted. They were not connected with the simple reporting that my father was doing for the *Guardian* at that time—he didn't like what he was doing. The ambitions were connected with what my father had done for the *Guardian* long before, in that past out of which he had so suddenly appeared to me.

My father had a bookcase-and-desk. It was a bulky piece of furniture, stained dark red and varnished, with glass doors to the three bookshelves, and a lipped, sloping, hinged lid to the desk. It was made from pine and packing crates (the raw, unstained side panel of one drawer was stencilled *Stow away from boilers*). It was part of the furniture my father had brought from where he had been living in the country. I was introduced to this furniture in Port of Spain, recognized it as my father's and therefore mine, and got to like each piece; in my grandmother's house in Chaguanas nothing had belonged to me.

Below the sloping lid of the desk, and in the square, long drawers, were my father's records: old papers, where silver fish squirmed and mice sometimes nested, with their pink young— to be thrown out into the yard for chickens to peck at. My father liked to keep documents. There were letters from a London writing school, letters from the *Guardian*. I read them all, many times, and always with pleasure, relishing them as things from the past; though the raised letter-heads meant more to me than the letters. There was a passport with my father's picture—a British passport, for someone from the colony of Trinidad and Tobago; this passport had never been used. And there was a big ledger in which my father had pasted his early writings for the *Guardian*. It was an estate wages ledger; the newspaper cuttings had been pasted over the names of the labourers and the wages they had been paid week by week.

This ledger became one of the books of my childhood. It was there, in the old-fashioned *Guardian* type and lay-out—and not in the paper that fell on the front steps every morning, sometimes while it was still dark—that I got to love the idea of newspapers and the idea of print.

I saw my father's name in print, in the two spellings, Naipal and Naipaul. I saw the pen-names that in those glorious days he had sometimes also used: Paul Nye, Paul Prye. He had written a lot, and I had no trouble understanding that the *Guardian* had been a better paper then. The Chaguanas that my father had written about was more full of excitement and stories than the Chaguanas I had known. The place seemed to have degenerated, with the paper.

My father had written about village feuds, family vendettas, murders, bitter election battles. (And how satisfying to see, in print, the names of those relations of my mother's whose ghostly election banners, from a subsequent election, I had seen on the verandah wall of my mother's family house!) My father had written about strange characters. Like the negro "hermit": once rich and pleasure-seeking, now penniless and living alone with a dog in a hut in the swamp-lands. The *Guardian* called my father's hermit Robinson Crusoe. Then, true to his new name, this Crusoe decided to go to Tobago, Crusoe's island; he intended to walk there; and, fittingly, there was no more about him. There was the negro woman of 112 who said she remembered the days of slavery when "negroes were lashed to poles and flogged." That didn't mean much; but the words (which made one of the headlines) stuck, because I didn't know that particular use of "lash."

My father had his own adventures. Once, on a rainy night, and far from home, his motorcycle skidded off the road and for some reason he had to spend the night up a tree. Was that true? I don't remember what my father said, but I understood that the story was exaggerated.

It didn't matter. I read the stories as stories; they were written by my father; I went back to them as to memorials of a heroic time I had missed. There was something about the ledger I noticed but never asked about, accepting it as a fact about the ledger: the clippings stopped quite suddenly; at least a third of the book remained unused.

In the *Guardian* that came to the house every day my father's name didn't appear. The style of the paper had changed; the reporting was all anonymous. The paper was part of the drama of the early morning, but I was interested in it only as a printed object. I didn't think to look for what my father had written.

The fact was I was too young for newspapers. I was old enough only for stories. The ledger in the desk was like a personal story. In it the ideas of "once upon a time" and my father's writing life in old Chaguanas came together and penetrated my imagination, together with Charles Kingsley's story of Perseus (a baby cast out to sea, a mother enslaved), which was the first story my father read to me; the early chapters of *Oliver Twist;* Mr. Murdstone from *David Copperfield;* Mr. Squeers. All this my father introduced me to. All this was added to my discovery of Port of Spain and the life of our street. It was the richest and most serene time of my childhood.

It didn't last long. It lasted perhaps for two years. My mother's mother decided to leave Chaguanas. She bought a cocoa estate of 350 acres in the hills to the north-west of Port of Spain, and it was decided—by the people in the family who decided on such matters—that the whole family, or all its dependent branches, should move there. My mother was willing enough to be with her family again. The rest of us were not so willing. But we had to go. We had to leave the house in Port of Spain. After the quiet and order of our two years as a separate unit we were returned to the hubbub of the extended family and our scattered nonentity within it.

The intention was good, even romantic. It was that the family should together work the rich and beautiful estate. It was more the idea of the commune than a continuation of the extended family life of Chaguanas, where most people had their own land and houses and used the family house as a centre. Here we all lived in the estate house. It was a big house, but it wasn't big enough; and the idea of communal labour turned out to be little more than the exaction of labour from the helpless.

In Chaguanas the family had been at the centre of a whole network of Hindu reverences. People were always coming to the Chaguanas house to pay their respects, to issue invitations or to bring gifts of food. Here we were alone. Unsupported by that Chaguanas world, with no one outside to instruct us in our obligations, even to ourselves, our own internal reverences began to go; our Hindu system began to fail.

There were desperate quarrels. Animosities and alliances shifted all the time; people had constantly to be looked at in new ways. Nothing was stable. Food was short; transport to Port of Spain difficult. I didn't see my father for days. His nerves deteriorated. He had been given one of the servant rooms (we children slept anywhere). In that room one Sunday evening, in a great rage, he threw a glass of hot milk. It cut me above my right eye; my eyebrow still shows the scar.

After two years we moved back to the house in Port of Spain, but only to some rooms in it. There was a period of calm, especially after my father got a job with the government and left the *Guardian*. But we were under pressure. More and more people from my mother's family were coming to Port of Spain, and we were squeezed into less and less space. The street itself had changed. On the reclaimed area of Docksite there was the American base; and at least one of the houses or yards had become a kind of brothel ground.

Disorder within, disorder without. Only my school life was ordered; anything that had happened there I could date at once. But my family life—my life at home or my life in the house, in the street—was jumbled, without sequence. The sequence I have given it here has come to me only with the writing of this piece. And that is why I am not sure whether it was before the upheaval of our move or after our return to Port of Spain that I became aware of my father writing stories.

In one of the drawers of the desk there was a typescript—on *Guardian* "copy" paper—of a story called "White Man's Way." It was an old story and it didn't mean much to me. A white overseer on a horse, a girl in a cane-field: I cannot remember what happened. I was at sea with this kind of story. For all my reputation in the house as a reader of books—and my interest in books and magazines as printed objects was genuine—there was an element of pretence, a carry-over from the schoolroom, in much of the reading I did on my own. It was easier for me to take an interest in what my father read to me. And my father never read this story aloud to me.

I remember that in the story there was a phrase about the girl's breasts below her bodice; and I suppose that my father had grafted his sexual yearnings on to an English or American magazine-style tropical story. In the desk, hoarded with his other papers, there was a stack of these magazines, often looked at by me, never really read. My father had done or partly done a correspondence course with a London writing school before the war—some of the letters were in the desk. The school had recommended a study of the "market." These magazines were the market.

But "White Man's Way" was in the past. The stories my father now began to write were aimed at no market. He wrote in fits and starts. He wrote in bed, with a pencil. He wrote slowly, with great patience: he could write the same paragraph over and over again. Liable to stomach pains, and just as liable to depressions (his calls then for "the Epictetus" or "the Marcus Aurelius," books of comfort, were like calls for his stomach medicine), my father became calm before and during his writing moods.

He didn't write a great deal. He wrote one long story and four or five shorter stories. In the shorter pieces my father, moving far from my mother's family and the family of his uncle by marriage, re-created his own background. The people he wrote about were poor, but that wasn't the point. These stories celebrated Indian village life, and the Hindu rituals that gave grace and completeness to that life. They also celebrated elemental things, the order of the working day, the labour of the rice-fields, the lighting of the cooking fire in the half-walled gallery of a thatched hut, the preparation and eating of food. There was very little "story" in these stories. But to me they gave a beauty (which in a corner of my mind still endures, like a fantasy of home) to the Indian village life I had never known. And when we went to the country to visit my father's own relations, who were the characters in these stories, it was like a fairytale came to life.

The long story was quite different. It was comic; yet it dealt with cruelty. It was the story of an Indian village thug. He is taken out of school at fourteen in order to be married: a boy of high caste, as the protagonist is, should be married before his whiskers grow. In the alien, Presbyterian school the boy is momentarily abashed by the idea of his early marriage; at home he is proud of the manhood this marriage confers. He terrorizes and beats his wife: strong men should beat their wives. Secure in his own eyes as a brahmin and the son of a landowner, he disdains work and seeks glory. He uses his father's money and authority to establish and lead a village stick-fighting group, though he himself has no skill in that exacting and elegant martial art. None of this is done for gain; it is all done for glory, a caste idea of manhood, a wish for battle, a wish to be a leader. The quality of the ambition is high; the village setting is petty. The would-be caste chieftain ends in the alien police courts as an uneducated country criminal, speaking broken English.

I was involved in the slow making of this story from the beginning to the end. Every new bit was read out to me, every little variation; and I read every new typescript my father made as the story grew. It was the greatest imaginative experience of my childhood. I knew the story by heart, yet always loved to read it or hear it, feeling a thrill at every familiar turn, ready for all the varied emotions. Growing up within my extended family, knowing nothing else, or looking at everything else from the outside, I had no social sense, no sense of other societies; and as a result, reading (mainly English books) was difficult for me. I couldn't enter worlds that were not like mine. I could get on only with the broadest kind of story, the fairytale. The world of this story of my father's was something I knew. To the pastoral beauty of his other stories it added cruelty, and comedy that made the cruelty just bearable. It was my private epic.

With the encouragement, and possibly the help, of my mother's elder brother, my father printed the stories. That was another excitement. And then somehow, without any discussion that I remember, it seemed to be settled, in my mind as well as my father's, that I was to be a writer.

On the American base at the end of the street the flag was raised every morning and lowered every evening; the bugle sounded twice a day. The street was full of Americans, very neat in their shiny starched uniforms. At night the soundtrack of the open-air American cinema thundered away. The man in the yard next door slaughtered a goat in his back gallery every Sunday morning and hung the red carcase up, selling pieces. This slaughtering of the goat was a boisterous business; the man next door, to attract customers, made it appear like a celebration of the holiday. And every morning he called out to the man in the servant room in our yard: "Bogart!" Fantasy calling to fantasy on our street. And in the two rooms to which we had been reduced, our fantasy was dizzier. I was eleven; I had given no sign of talent; but I was to be a writer.

On the window frame beside his bed, where he did his writing, my father had hung a framed picture of O. Henry, cut out from the jacket of the Hodder and Stoughton uniform edition. "O. Henry, the greatest short story writer the world has ever known." All that I know of this writer to this day are the three stories my father read to me. One was "The Gift of the Magi," a story of two poor lovers who, to buy gifts for each other, make sacrifices that render the gifts useless. The second story (as I remember it) was about a tramp who decides in a dream to reform and then wakes up to find a policeman about to arrest him. The third story—about a condemned man waiting to be electrocuted—was unfinished; O. Henry died while writing it. That unfinished story made an impression on me, as did the story of O. Henry's own death. He had asked for the light to be kept on and had spoken a line from a popular song: "I don't want to go home in the dark."

Poverty, cheated hopes and death: those were the associations of the framed picture beside my father's bed. From the earliest stories and bits of stories my father had read to me, before the upheaval of the move, I had arrived at the conviction—the conviction that is at the root of so much human anguish and passion, and corrupts so many lives—that there was justice in the world. The wish to be a writer was a development of that. To be a writer as O. Henry was, to die in mid-sentence, was to triumph over darkness. And like a wild religious faith that hardens in adversity, this wish to be a writer, this refusal to be extinguished, this wish to seek at some future time for justice, strengthened as our conditions grew worse in the house on the street.

Our last two years in that house—our last two years in the extended family—were very bad indeed. At the end of 1946, when I was fourteen, my father managed to buy his own house. By that time my childhood was over; I was fully made.

THE WISH to be a writer didn't go with a wish or a need actually to write. It went only with the idea I had been given of the writer, a fantasy of nobility. It was something that lay ahead, and outside the life I knew—far from family and clan, city, colony, *Trinidad Guardian*, negroes.

In 1948 I won a Trinidad government scholarship. These scholarships were meant to give a man a profession and they could last for seven years. I decided to use mine to do English at Oxford. I didn't want a degree; I wanted only to get away; and I thought that in my three or four scholarship years at Oxford my talent would somehow be revealed, and the books would start writing themselves.

My father had written little. I was aware now of the trouble he had finding things to write about. He had read little, was only a dipper—I never knew him to read a book through. His idea of the writer—as a person triumphant and detached—was a private composite of O. Henry, Warwick Deeping, Marie Corelli (of the *Sorrows of Satan*), Charles Dickens, Somerset Maugham, and J. R. Ackerley (of *Hindoo Holiday*). My own reading was not much better. My inability to understand other societies made nonsense of the Huxley and the D. H. Lawrence and the Evelyn Waugh I tried to read, and even of the Stendhal I had read at school. And I had written scarcely at all. If the O. Henry trick ending stood in the way of my father's writing, Huxley and Lawrence and Waugh made me feel I had no material. But it had been settled that I was to be a writer. That was the career I was travelling to.

I left Trinidad in 1950. It was five years later, in the BBC freelances' room, that I thought to write of the shout of "Bogart!" That shout came from a tormented time. But that was not how I remembered it. My family circumstances had been too confused; I preferred not to focus on them; in my mind they had no sequence. My narrator, recording the life of his street, was as serene as I had been when we had first moved to Port of Spain with my father.

At the end of the book my narrator left his street. *I left them all and walked briskly towards the aeroplane, not looking back, looking only at my shadow before me, a dancing dwarf on the tarmac.* That line, the last in the book, wrote itself. It held memories of the twelve years, no more, I had spent with my father. The movement of the shadows of trees and houses across the street—more dramatic to me than the amorphous shadows of Chaguanas—was one of the first things I had noticed in Port of Spain. And it was with that sudden churlishness, a sudden access of my own hysteria, that I had left my father in 1950, not looking back. I wish I had. I might have taken away, and might still possess, some picture of him on that day. He died miserably—back at the tormenting *Guardian*—three years later.

To become a writer, that noble thing, I had thought it necessary to leave. Actually to write, it was necessary to go back. It was the beginning of self-knowledge.

3

IN 1977, after twenty-seven years, I saw Bogart again. He hadn't been important in our family; he had always liked to hide; and for more than twenty years I had had no news of him. I had grown to think of him as a vanished person, one of the many I had left behind for good when I left Trinidad.

Then I discovered that he too had left Trinidad, and not long after I had left, not long after I had done the sign for his tailoring shop in Carenage. He had gone to Venezuela. There he had been for all this time. As a child, considering his disappearances and returns, I had divined his dreams (because they were also partly mine) of sensual fulfillment in another land and another language. And then, in the story I had devised for him in one afternoon, I had cruelly made him a bigamist. He had been part of my luck as a writer. My ignorance of his true story had been part of that luck. I had been free to simplify and work fast.

I was going now, in 1977, to spend some weeks in Venezuela. And when I passed through Trinidad I tried to get Bogart's address. That wasn't easy. He still apparently caused embarrassment to his close relations. And then there was some confusion about the address itself. The first address I was given was in the oil town of Maracaibo, in the west. The second was on the former pearl island of Margarita, three or four hundred miles to the east, on the Caribbean coast. That was like the old Bogart: a man on the move. He seemed, from this second address, to be in business in Margarita, as "international traders" or an "international trading corporation" or an "import-export corporation."

Venezuela was rich, with its oil. Trinidad was now also rich, with the oil that had been discovered off-shore. But when I was a child Trinidad was poor, even with the American bases; and Venezuela was a place to which people like Bogart tried to go.

Many went illegally. In a fishing boat it was a passage of a few hours, no more than a drift with the strong current, across the southern mouth of the Gulf of Paria. In the mixed population of the villages in the Orinoco delta, far from authority, Trinidadians who were protected could pass. Some acquired Venezuelan birth certificates; so it happened that men whose grandfathers had come from India sank into the personalities, randomly issued by the migration brokers, of Spanish mulattoes named Morales or García or Ybarra.

These men didn't go only for the money. They went for the adventure. Venezuela was the Spanish language, South America: a continent. Trinidad was small, an island, a British colony. The maps in our geography books, concentrating on British islands in the Caribbean, seemed to stress our smallness and isolation. In the map of Trinidad, the map which I grew to carry in my head, Venezuela was an unexplained little peninsula in the top left-hand corner.

True knowledge of geography, and with it a sense of historical wonder, began to come sixteen years after I had left Trinidad, when for two years I worked on a history of the region. For those two years—reading in the British Museum, the Public Record Office, the London Library—I lived with the documents of our region, seeking to detach the region from big historical "over-views," trying only to understand how my corner of the New World, once indeed new, and capable of developing in any number of ways, had become the place it was.

I saw the Gulf of Paria with the eyes of the earliest explorers and officials: I saw it as an aboriginal Indian lake, busy with canoes, sometimes of war. To those Indians, crossing easily back and forth, Trinidad was Venezuela in small. There was a mighty Caroni river in Venezuela; there was a small Caroni, a stream, in Trinidad. There was a Chaguaramas in Trinidad; there was a Chaguaramas in Venezuela.

Trinidad sat in the mouth of the Orinoco, beyond the "drowned lands" of the delta that Sir Walter Raleigh saw: now a refuge for people from the mainland, now a base for attack. To the Spaniards Trinidad guarded the river that led to El Dorado. When that fantasy faded, all that province of El Dorado—Trinidad and Guiana and the drowned lands—was left to bush. But the Indians were ground down. One day in the British Museum I found out about the name of my birthplace Chaguanas.

Raleigh's last, lunatic raid on "El Dorado" had taken place in 1617. Eight years later the Spaniards were settling accounts with the local Indians. On 12 October 1625 the King of Spain wrote to the Governor of Trinidad: "I asked you to give me some information about a certain nation of Indians called Chaguanes, who you say are above one thousand and of such bad disposition that it was they who led the English when they captured the town. Their crime hasn't been punished because forces were not available for this purpose and because the Indians acknowledge no master save their own will. You have decided to give them a punishment. Follow the rules I have given you; and let me know how you get on."

I felt that I was the first person since the seventeenth century to whom that document had spoken directly. A small tribe, one among hundreds—they had left behind only their name. The Chaguanas I knew was an Indian country town, Indian of India. Hindi-speaking Indians had simplified the name into a Hindu caste name, Chauhan. It had its Hindu districts and its Muslim districts; it had the religious and caste rivalries of India. It was where my mother's father had bought many acres of cane-land and rice-land and where he had built his Indian-style house. It was also where, from a reading of my father's stories of village life, I had set my fantasy of home, my fantasy of things as they were at the very beginning: the ritualized day, fields and huts, the mango tree in the yard, the simple flowers, the lighting of fires in the evening.

Trinidad I knew too well. It was, profoundly, part of my past. That past lay over the older past; and I couldn't, when I was in Trinidad again, see it as the setting of the aboriginal history I knew and had written about. But I had written about Venezuela and its waters without having seen them. The historical Venezuela—as it existed in my imagination—was vivid to me. And, when I went on to Venezuela from Trinidad in 1977, all that I saw as the aeroplane tilted away from the island was fresh and hallowed, the land and sea of the earliest travellers: the great froth-fringed stain of the Orinoco on the Gulf, the more local, muddier stains of small rivers from the Paria Peninsula (the unexplained peninsula in the left-hand corner of the school map of Trinidad). In 1604, sixteen years after the defeat of the Spanish Armada he had led against England, the Duke of Medina Sidonia had been sent here by the King of Spain, to report on the best way of defending this coast and especially the salt-pans of Araya (into which the Paria Peninsula ran, after 150 miles). Such a task! (And, when I got to know it later, such a desolation still, Araya, on its Caribbean coast: thorn trees and cactus in a hummocked red desert beside the murky sea, life only in the long, slack waves, the vultures in the sky, and the pelicans, all beak and belly and wings, undisturbed on their rock-perches.)

To land at La Guaira airport, on the Venezuelan coast, was to come down to a different country. Scores of bulldozers were levelling the red earth to extend the airport. There were yachts in the marina beside the big resort hotel. The highway that led to Caracas in its inland valley had for stretches been tunnelled through the mountains.

Venezuela was rich. But in its oil economy many of its people were superfluous. The restaurants of the capital were Spanish or Italian, the hotels American. The technicians in the industrial towns that were being built in the interior were European;

people spoke of a second Spanish conquest. Oil money—derived from foreign machines, foreign markets—fed a real-estate boom in the towns. Agriculture was neglected; it was like something from the poor past. The descendants of the people who had been brought in long ago to restock the Indian land, to work the plantations, were no longer needed. Still pure negro in the cocoa areas (fragrant with the scent of vanilla), old mulatto mixtures elsewhere, they had been abandoned with the plantations. And to travel out to the countryside was to see—on a continental scale—a kind of peasant dereliction that had vanished from Trinidad: shacks and a few fruit trees in small yards, rough little road-side stalls offering fruit from the yards.

It was in a setting like that, on the island of Margarita, in a setting close to what he had known in Trinidad, when I had painted the sign for him at Carenage, that I found Bogart.

Columbus had given Margarita its name, "the pearl." It was across the sea from Araya, and early maps magnified its size. Pearl diving had used up the Indians fast; and there were no pearls now. Margarita lived as a resort island and a duty-free zone: Venezuelans flew over from the mainland to shop. Half the island was desert, as red as Araya; half was green.

Bogart was in the green part. I had imagined, because I had understood he was in the import-export business, that he would be in one of the little towns. He was in a village, far from town or beach. It took some finding—and then suddenly in mid-afternoon, a glaring, shadowless time, in a dusty rural lane, very local, with no sign of resort life or duty-free activity, I was there: little houses, corrugated-iron shacks, open yards, fruit trees growing out of blackened, trampled earth, their promise of a little bounty adding (to me, who had known such places as a child) to the feeling of dirt and poverty and empty days.

Bogart's shop was a little concrete-walled building. Without the big sign painted on the wall I might have missed it. The two brown doors of the shop were closed. The side gate to the yard was closed. In the open yard to one side, in an unwalled shed attached as extra living space to an old, two-roomed wooden house, a bent old woman, not white, not brown, was taking her ease on a wooden bench: kerchiefed, long-skirted, too old now for a siesta, existing at that moment only in a daze of heat, dullness and old age: pans and plates on a table beside her, potted plants on the ground.

I banged for a long time on Bogart's side gate. At last it opened: a mulatto girl of fifteen or sixteen or seventeen held it open. The old woman next door was swaddled in her long skirt; the light, loose frock of this girl was like the merest covering over her hard little body, and she was in slippers, someone at ease, someone at home. She was pale brown, well-fed, with an oval face.

The questioning in her eyes vanished when she saw the taxi in the road. Her demeanour moderated, but only slightly, into that of the servant. She let me in without a word and then seemed to stand behind me. So that any idea that she might be Bogart's daughter left me, and I thought of her as one of the unneeded, one of the many thousands littered in peasant yards and cast out into the wilderness of Venezuela.

The dirt yard over which the girl had walked in slippers was smooth and swept. At the back of the shop, and at a right angle to it, was a row of two or three rooms with a wide verandah all the way down. From one of these rooms Bogart soon appeared, dressing fast: I had interrupted his siesta. So that, though he was now a man of sixty or more, he was as I had remembered him: heavy-lidded, sleepy. He used to have a smoothness of skin and softness of body that suggested he might become fat. He still had the skin and the softness, but he hadn't grown any fatter.

He called me by the name used by my family. I had trouble with his. I had grown up calling him by the Hindi word for a maternal uncle. That didn't seem suitable now; but I couldn't call him by his name either. In that moment of greeting and mutual embarrassment the girl disappeared.

He had got my telegram, he said; and he had sent a telegram

in reply—but I hadn't got that. He didn't ask me into any of the back rooms or even the verandah. He opened up the back door of the shop. He seated me facing the dark shop—stocked mainly with cloth. He sat facing the bright yard. Even after twenty-seven years, I clearly wasn't to stay long.

His voice was gruffer, but there was no trace of Venezuela in his English accent. The light from the yard showed his puffy, sagging cheeks and the black interstices of his teeth. That mouthful of apparently rotten teeth weakened his whole face and gave a touch of inanity to his smile.

His subject, after routine family inquiries, was himself. He never asked what I had done with my life, or even what I was doing in Venezuela. Like many people who live in small or retarded communities, he had little curiosity. His own life was his only story. But that was what I wanted to hear.

When he was a young man, during the war, he said, he had made a trip to Venezuela. He had become involved with a local woman. To his great alarm, she had had a child for him.

Bogart said, "But you knew that."

I didn't know it. Nothing had been said about Bogart's misadventure. Our family kept its secrets well.

For some years after that he had divided his time between Trinidad and Venezuela, freedom and the woman. Finally— since there was no job for him in Trinidad—he had settled in Venezuela. He had got a job with an oil company, and there he had stayed. That was the let-down for me: that Bogart, the adventurer, with his own idea of the Spanish Main, should have lived a life of routine for twenty-five years. He would still have been in that job, he said, if it hadn't been for a malevolent negro. The negro, raised to a little authority and rendered vicious, tormented him. In the end Bogart left the job, with a reduced gratuity. He was glad to leave. That life hadn't really been satisfactory, he said. The woman hadn't been satisfactory. His children had been a disappointment; they were not bright.

Not bright! This judgment, from Bogart! It was astonishing

that he could go back to an old way of thinking, that he could create this picture of his Venezuelan family as mulatto nondescripts. But he was also saying, obliquely, that he had left his wife and children on the mainland and had come to the island to make a fresh start. That explained the confusion about the two addresses. It also explained the demeanour of the mulatto girl, who wasn't allowed to appear again.

He had been part of my luck as a writer; his simplicity had been part of that luck. Even as a child, I had divined his impulses. He wasn't a bigamist, as I had made him in my story. But he had been caught by the senses; and now in old age he was seeking again the liberation he had been looking for when he had come to our street in Port of Spain.

But he was old now. He had begun to have some sense of life as an illusion, and his thoughts were turning to higher things—they had begun to turn that way when he was having trouble with the negro. He didn't know how to pray, he said. He had never paid attention to the pundits—he spoke apologetically, addressing me as someone whose family was full of pundits. But every morning, before he ate, he bathed and sat cross-legged and for half an hour he took the name of Rama—Rama, the Indo-Aryan epic hero, the embodiment of virtue, God himself, the name Gandhi had spoken twice, after he had been shot.

After telling his story, old family graces seemed to return to Bogart. He hadn't offered hospitality; now he offered anything in his shop. Shoddy goods, for the local market. I took a scarf, synthetic, lightweight material. And then it was close to opening time, and time for me to go.

Outside, I studied the lettering on the shop wall. The paint was new; the sign-writer's rules and pencil outlines were still visible. Perhaps the sign I had done for him twenty-seven or twenty-eight years before had given him the taste for signs. This one was very big. *Grandes Rebajas! Aprovéchese!* "Big Reductions! Don't Miss Them!" The Spanish language: no romance in these workaday words now.

He had lived the life of freedom, and it had taken him back almost to where he had been in the beginning. But though he appeared not to know it, the Hindu family life he had wanted to escape from—the life of our extended family, our clan—had disintegrated in Trinidad. The family Bogart had known in my grandmother's house in Port of Spain—neutered men, oppressed and cantankerous women, uneducated children—had scattered, and changed. To everyone there had come the wish to break away; and the disintegration of our private Hindu world—in all, we were fifty cousins—had released energy in people who might otherwise have remained passive. Many of my cousins, starting late, acquired professions, wealth; some migrated to more demanding lands.

For all its physical wretchedness and internal tensions, the life of the clan had given us all a start. It had given us a caste certainty, a high sense of the self. Bogart had escaped too soon; still passive, he had settled for nullity. Now, discovering his desolation, he was turning to religion, something that he thought was truly his own. He had only memories to guide him. His memories were not of sacred books and texts, but rituals, forms. So he could think only of bathing in the mornings, sitting in a certain posture, and speaking the name of Rama. It was less a wish for religion and old ritual, less a wish for the old life than a wish, in the emptiness of his Venezuela, for the consolation of hallowed ways.

Thinking of him, I remembered something I had seen eight years before in Belize, south of Yucatán, near the great ancient Mayan site of Altun Ha. The site, a complex of temples spread over four square miles, had been abandoned some centuries before the coming of the Spaniards. The steep-stepped temples had become forested hills; and in the forest beside the main road there were still many unexcavated small hills, hard to see unless you were looking for them.

The priests of Altun Ha had been killed perhaps a thousand years before; there might have been a peasant uprising. That was the theory of the Canadian archaeologist who was living on the site in a tent marked with the name of his university. Not far away, on the edge of a government camp beside a stream, a Mayan peasant was building a hut. He had put up the pillars—trimmed tree-branches—and the roof-frame. Now he was marking out the boundary of his plot. It was an act that called for some ritual, and the man was walking along the boundary, swinging smoking copal in a wicker censer, and muttering. He was making up his own incantation. The words were gibberish.

When I got back to Caracas I found the telegram Bogart said he had sent me. *Sorry but your visit not possible now Am in and out all the time these days It's me alone here in Margarita.*

4

THE LOCAL history I studied at school was not interesting. It offered so little. It was like the maps in the geography books that stressed the islands and virtually did away with the continent. We were a small part of somebody else's "overview": we were part first of the Spanish story, then of the British story. Perhaps the school histories could be written in no other way. We were, after all, a small agricultural colony; and we couldn't say we had done much. (The current "revolutionary" or Africanist overview is not an improvement: it is no more than the old imperialist attitude turned inside out.) To discover the wonder of our situation as children of the New World we had to look into ourselves; and to someone from my kind of Hindu background that wasn't easy.

I grew up with two ideas of history, almost two ideas of time. There was history with dates. That kind of history affected people and places abroad, and my range was wide: ancient Rome (the study of which, during my last two years at Queen's Royal College in Port of Spain, was the most awakening part of

my formal education); nineteenth-century England; the nationalist movement in India.

But Chaguanas, where I was born, in an Indian-style house
my grandfather had built, had no dates. If I read in a book that
Gandhi had made his first call for civil disobedience in India in
1919, that date seemed recent. But 1919, in Chaguanas, in the life
of the Indian community, was almost unimaginable. It was a
time beyond recall, mythical. About our family, the migration
of our ancestors from India, I knew only what I knew or what I
was told. Beyond (and sometimes even within) people's memories was undated time, historical darkness. Out of that darkness
(extending to place as well as to time) we had all come. The
India where Gandhi and Nehru and the others operated was historical and real. The India from which we had come was impos-
sibly remote, almost as imaginary as the land of the *Ramayana*,
our Hindu epic. I lived easily with that darkness, that lack of
knowledge. I never thought to inquire further.

My mother's father had built a big house in Chaguanas. I
didn't know when. (It was in 1920; I was given that date in
1972.) He had gone back to India and died—in the life of our
family, a mythical event. (It occurred in 1926.) Little by little I
understood that this grandfather still had relations in India, that
there was a village, with an actual address. My mother, giving
me this address in 1961, recited it like poetry: district, sub-district,
village.

In 1962, at the end of a year of travel in India, I went to that
village. I wasn't prepared for the disturbance I felt, turning off
from the India where I had been a traveller, and driving in a
government jeep along a straight, dusty road to another, very
private world. Two ideas of history came together during that
short drive, two ways of thinking about myself.

And there I discovered that to my grandfather this village—
the pond, the big trees he would have remembered, the brick
dwellings with their enclosed courtyards (unlike the adobe and

thatch of Trinidad Indian villages), the fields in the flat land, the immense sky, the white shrines—this village was the real place. Trinidad was the interlude, the illusion.

My grandfather had done well in Trinidad. He had bought much land—I continue to discover "pieces" he had bought; he had bought properties in Port of Spain; he had established a very large family and in our community he had a name. But he was willing, while he was still an active man, to turn his back on this and return home, to the real place. He hadn't gone alone—a family secret suddenly revealed: he had taken another woman with him. But my grandfather hadn't seen his village again; he had died on the train from Calcutta. The woman with him had made her way to the village (no doubt reciting the address I had heard my mother recite). And there for all these years, in the house of my grandfather's brother, she had stayed.

She was very old when I saw her. Her skin had cracked; her eyes had filmed over; she moved about the courtyard on her haunches. She still had a few words of English. She had photographs of our family—things of Trinidad—to show; there remained to her the curious vanity that she knew us all very well.

She had had a great adventure. But her India had remained intact; her idea of the world had remained whole; no other idea of reality had broken through. It was different for thousands of others. In July and August 1932, during my father's first spell on the *Trinidad Guardian* (and around the time I was born), one of the big running stories in the paper was the repatriation of Indian immigrants on the S.S. *Ganges*.

Indian immigrants, at the end of their contract, were entitled to a small grant of land or to a free trip back to India with their families. The promise hadn't always been kept. Many Indians, after they had served out their indenture, had found themselves destitute and homeless. Such people, even within my memory, slept at night in the Port of Spain squares. Then in 1931 the *Ganges* had come, and taken away more than a thousand. Only "paupers" were taken free; everyone else had to pay a small fare. The news, in 1932, that the *Ganges* was going to come again created frenzy in those who had been left behind the previous year. They saw this second coming of the *Ganges* as their last chance to go home, to be released from Trinidad. Many more wanted to go than could be taken on. A thousand left; a quarter were officially "paupers." Seven weeks later the *Ganges* reached Calcutta. And there, to the terror of the passengers, the *Ganges* was stormed by hundreds of derelicts, previously repatriated, who wanted now to be taken back to the other place. India for these people had been a dream of home, a dream of continuity after the illusion of Trinidad. All the India they had found was the area around the Calcutta docks.

Our own past was, like our idea of India, a dream. Of my mother's father, so important to our family, I grew up knowing very little. Of my father's family and my father's childhood I knew almost nothing. My father's father had died when my father was a baby. My father knew only his mother's stories of this man: a miserly and cruel man who counted every biscuit in the tin, made her walk five miles in the hot sun to save a penny fare, and, days before my father was born, drove her out of the house. My father never forgave his father. He forgave him only in a story he wrote, one of his stories of Indian village life, in which his mother's humiliation is made good by the ritual celebration of the birth of her son.

Another incident I knew about—and my father told this as a joke—was that at one time he had almost gone back to India on an immigrant ship. The family had been "passed" for repatriation; they had gone to the immigration depot on Nelson Island. There my father had panicked, had decided that he didn't want to go back to India. He hid in one of the latrines overhanging the sea, and he stayed there until his mother changed her mind about the trip back to India.

This was what my father passed on to me about his family and his childhood. The events were as dateless as the home events of my own confused childhood. His early life seemed an extension back in time of my own; and I did not think to ask until much later for a more connected narrative. When I was at Oxford I pressed him in letters to write an autobiography. This was to encourage him as a writer, to point him to material he had never used. But some deep hurt or shame, something still raw and unresolved in his experience, kept my father from attempting any autobiographical writing. He wrote about other members of his family. He never wrote about himself.

It wasn't until 1972, when I was forty, and nearly twenty years after my father's death, that I got a connected idea of his ancestry and early life.

I was in Trinidad. In a Port of Spain shop one day the Indian boy who sold me a paper said he was related to me. I was interested, and asked him how—the succeeding generations, spreading through our small community, had added so many relations to those I had known. He said, quickly and precisely, that he was the grandson of my father's sister. The old lady was dying, he said. I should try to see her soon. I went the next morning.

Thirty years before, her house in the open country near Chaguanas had been one of the fairytale places my father had taken me to: the thatched hut with its swept yard, its mango tree, its hibiscus hedge, and with fields at the back. My father had written a story about her. But it was a long time before I understood that the story had been about her; that the story—again, a story of ritual and reconciliation—was about her unhappy first marriage; and that her life in that fairytale hut with her second husband, a man of a low, cultivator caste, was wretched.

That was now far in the past. Even the kind of countryside I associated with her had vanished, been built over. She was dying in a daughter's house on the traffic-choked Eastern Main Road that led out of Port of Spain, in a cool, airy room made neat both for her death and for visitors. She was attended by children and grandchildren, people of varying levels of education and skill; some had been to Canada. Here, as everywhere else in Trinidad, there had been movement: my father's sister, at the end of her life, could see success.

She was very small, and had always been very thin. Uncovered by blanket or sheet, in a long blue nightdress and a new, white, too-big cardigan, she lay very light, like an object carefully placed, on her spring mattress, over which the sheet had been pulled smooth and tight.

The cardigan, in the tropical morning, was odd. It was like a baby's garment, put on for her by someone else; like a tribute to her death, like the extravagant gift of a devoted daughter; and also like the old lady's last attempt at a joke. Like my father, whom she resembled, she had always been a humorist in a gathering (the gloom, the irritation, came immediately afterwards); and this death chamber was full of chatter and easy movement. There was even a camera; and she posed, willingly. One man, breezing in, sat down so hard on the bed that the old lady bumped up; and it seemed to be one of her jokes.

But her talk to me was serious. It was of caste and blood. When I was a child we hadn't been able to talk. I could follow Hindi but couldn't speak it. She couldn't speak a word of English, though nearly everyone around her was bilingual. She had since picked up a little English; and her death-bed talk, of caste and blood, was in this broken language. The language still strained her, but what she was saying was like her bequest to me. I had known her poor, living with a man of a cultivator caste. She wanted me to know now, before the knowledge vanished with her, what she—and my father—had come from. She wanted me to know that the blood was good.

She didn't talk of her second husband. She talked of the first. He had treated her badly, but what was important about him now was that he was a Punjabi brahmin, a "scholar," she said, a man who could read and write Urdu and Persian. When she spoke of her father, she didn't remember the miserliness and cruelty which my father remembered. She wanted me to know that her father lived in a "galvanize" house—a galvanized-iron roof being a sign of wealth, unlike thatch, which was what had sheltered her for most of her life.

Her father was a pundit, she said. And he was fussy; he didn't like having too much to do with the low. And here—since her face was too old to be moulded into any expression save one of great weariness—the old lady used her shrivelled little hand to make a gentle gesture of disdain. The disdain was for the low among Hindus. My father's sister had spent all her life in Trinidad; but in her caste vision no other community mattered or properly existed.

She took the story back to her father's mother. This was as far as her memory went. And for me it was far enough. With no dates, and no big external events to provide historical markers, I found it hard to hold this relationship in my head. But this story contained many of my father's sister's other stories; and it gave me something like a family history. In one detail it was shocking; but it all came to me as a fairy story. And I shall reconstruct it here as a story—momentarily keeping the characters at a distance.

About 1880, in the ancient town of Ayodhya in the United Provinces in India, a young girl of the Parray clan gave birth to a son. She must have been deeply disgraced, because she was willing to go alone with her baby to a far-off island to which other people of the region were going. That was how the Parray woman came to Trinidad. She intended her son to be a pundit; and in the district of Diego Martin she found a good pundit who was willing to take her son in and instruct him. (There was no hint, in the tale I heard, of sugar estates and barracks and contract labour.)

The years passed. The boy went out into the world and began to do pundit's work. He also dealt, in a small way, in the goods Hindus used in religious ceremonies. His mother began to look for a bride for him. Women of suitable caste and clan were not easy to find in Trinidad, but the Parray woman had some luck. It happened that three brothers of a suitable clan had made the journey out from India together, and it happened that one of these brothers had seven daughters.

The Parray boy married one of these daughters. They had three children, a girl and two boys. They lived in the village of Cunupia, not far from Chaguanas, in a house with adobe walls and a galvanized-iron roof. Quite suddenly, when the youngest child, a boy, was only two, the young Parray fell ill and died. Somehow all the gold coins he had hoarded disappeared; and the aunts and uncles thought the children and their mother should be sent back to India. Arrangements were made, but then at the last moment the youngest child didn't want to go. He ran away and hid in a latrine, and the ship sailed without them.

The family was scattered. The eldest child, a girl, worked in the house of a relative; she never learned to read or write. The elder boy went out to work on the sugar estates for eight cents a day. The younger boy was spared for school. He was sent to stay with his mother's sister, who had married a man who owned a shop and was starting a bus company. The boy went to school by day and worked until late at night in the shop.

The Parray woman lived on for some time, mourning her pundit son, whom she had brought from India as a baby. She always wore white for grief, and she became known in the country town of Chaguanas: a very small, even a dwarfish, woman with white hair and a pale complexion. She walked with a stick, and passed for a witch. Children mocked her; sometimes, as she approached, people drew the sign of the cross on the road.

The Parray woman was my father's grandmother. The Parray man who died young was my father's father. The elder boy who went out to work in the cane-fields became a small farmer; when he was old he would cry at the memory of those eight cents a day. The younger boy who was spared for school—in order that he might become a pundit and so fufil the family destiny—was my father.

It is only in this story that I find some explanation of how, coming from that background, with little education and little

English, in a small agricultural colony where writing was not an occupation, my father developed the ambition to be a writer. It was a version of the pundit's vocation. When I got to know my father—in Port of Spain, in 1938, when he was thirty-two and I was six—he was a journalist. I took his occupation for granted. It was years before I worked back to a proper wonder at his achievement.

5

THE MANAGING editor of the *Trinidad Guardian* from 1929 to April 1934 was Gault MacGowan. I heard his name often when I was a child: he was the good man who had helped in the early days, and I was told that I had been shown to him as a baby one day in Chaguanas.

The Hindu who wants to be a pundit has first to find a guru. My father, wanting to learn to write, found MacGowan. It was MacGowan, my father said, who had taught him how to write; and all his life my father had for MacGowan the special devotion which the Hindu has for his guru. Even when I was at Oxford my father, in his letters to me, was passing on advice he had received twenty years before from MacGowan. In 1951 he wrote: "And as to a writer being hated or liked—I think it's the other way to what you think: a man is doing his work well when people begin *liking* him. I have never forgotten what Gault MacGowan told me years ago: 'Write sympathetically'; and this, I suppose, in no way prevents us from writing truthfully, even brightly."

MacGowan seems to have understood the relationship. In a letter he wrote me out of the blue in 1963, nearly thirty years after he had left Trinidad—a letter of pure affection, written to me as my father's son—MacGowan, then nearly seventy, living in Munich and "still publishing," said he had always been interested in the people of India. He had found my father willing to learn, and had gone out of his way to instruct him.

An unlikely bond between the two men was a mischievous sense of humour. "Trinidad Hangman Disappointed—Robbed of Fee by Executive Council—Bitter Regret." That was a Mac-Gowan headline over a news item about a condemned man's reprieve. It was the kind of joke my father also relished. That particular headline was brought up in court, as an example of MacGowan's irresponsibility, during one of the two big court cases MacGowan had in Trinidad. MacGowan said, "Doesn't the headline tell the story? I think that just the word 'robbed' is out of place." Publicity like this wasn't unwelcome to Mac-Gowan. He seems to have been litigious, and as a Fleet Street man he had the Fleet Street idea that a newspaper should every day in some way be its own news.

He had been brought out from England to Trinidad, on the recommendation of *The Times,* to modernize the *Trinidad Guardian.* The *Port of Spain Gazette,* founded in 1832, and representing French creole planter and business interests, was the established local paper. The *Guardian,* started in 1917, and representing other business interests, was floundering a long way behind. Its make-up was antiquated: on the front page a rectangle of closely printed news cables was set in a big frame of shop advertisements.

MacGowan changed the front page. He gave the *Guardian* a London look. He had a London feeling for international news ("Daily at Dawn—Last Night's News in London"). And to the affairs of multi-racial Trinidad he brought what, in local journalism, was absolutely new: a tourist's eye. Everything was worth looking at; there was a story in almost everything. And there were real excitements: French fugitives from Devil's Island, voodoo in negro backyards, Indian obeah, Venezuelan vampire bats (at one time the *Guardian* saw them flying about in daylight everywhere, and this concern with bats was to get both

MacGowan and my father into trouble). Every community interested MacGowan. The Indians of the countryside were cut off by language, religion and culture from the rest of the colonial population. MacGowan became interested in them—as material, and also as potential readers.

It was as an Indian voice, a reforming, "controversial" Indian voice ("Trinidad Indians Are Not Sincere"), that my father began to appear in MacGowan's *Guardian,* doing an occasional column signed "The Pundit." My feeling now is that these columns must have been rewritten by MacGowan, or (though my mother says no) that some of the material was plagiarized by my father from the reformist Hindu literature he had begun to read.

But a relationship was established between the two men. And my father—at a starting salary of four dollars a week—began to do reporting. There the voice was his own, the knowledge of Trinidad Indian life was his own; and the zest—for news, for the drama of everyday life, for human oddity—the zest for looking with which MacGowan infected him became real. He developed fast.

Even when there was no news, there could be news. "Chaguanas Man Writes Lindbergh—'I Know Where Your Baby Is.'" "Indians Pray for Gandhi—Despair in Chaguanas."

It must have been MacGowan who suggested to my father that everybody had a story. Was that really so? Not far from my mother's family house in Chaguanas was the railway crossing. Twice or four times a day an old one-armed negro closed and opened the gates. Did that man have a story? The man himself didn't seem to think so. He lived in absolute harmony with the long vacancies of his calling, and the brightest thing about my father's piece was MacGowan's headline: "Thirty-six Years of Watching a Trinidad Railway Gate."

More rewarding was the Indian shopkeeper a couple of houses down on the other side of the road. He was a man of the merchant caste who had come out to Trinidad as an indentured labourer. Field labour, and especially "heading" manure, carrying baskets of manure on his head, like untouchables in India, had been a humiliation and a torment to him. In the beginning he had cried at night; and sometimes his day's "task" so wore him out that he couldn't cook his evening meal. Once he had eaten a piece of sugar-cane in the field, and he had been fined a dollar, almost a week's wage. But he had served out his five-year indenture, and his caste instincts had reasserted themselves. He had made money as a merchant and was soon to build one of the earliest cinemas in the countryside. It was a good story; in Trinidad at that time, only my father could have done it.

MacGowan increased the circulation of the *Guardian*. But the directors of the paper had other local business interests as well, and they felt that MacGowan was damaging these interests. MacGowan, fresh from the depression in England, wanted to run a "Buy British" campaign; the chairman of the *Guardian* directors owned a trading company which dealt in American goods. The chairman had land at Macqueripe Bay; MacGowan campaigned for a road to Maracas Bay, where the chairman had no land. Some of the directors had invested in tourist ventures; MacGowan was running stories in the *Guardian* about "mad bats" that flew about in daylight, and his cables to *The Times* and *New York Times* about vampire bats and a special Trinidad form of rabies were said to be frightening away cruise ships.

Paralytic rabies was, in fact, killing cattle in Trinidad at this time. And for all the playfulness of his "mad bat" campaign ("Join the Daylight Bat Hunt—Be First"), MacGowan was acting on good advice. A local French creole doctor had recently established the link between bats and paralytic rabies, and was experimenting with a vaccine; the work of this doctor, Pawan, was soon to be acknowledged in text books of tropical medicine. But the *Guardian* chairman, who said later he had never heard of anyone in Trinidad dying from a bat bite, decided that MacGowan had to go.

MacGowan couldn't be sacked; he had his contract. He

could, however, be attacked; and the editor of the *Port of Spain Gazette,* whom MacGowan had often satirized, was only too willing to help. "Scaremongering MacGowan Libels Trinidad in Two Continents": this was a headline in the *Gazette* one day. MacGowan sued and won. Journalistically, the case was also a triumph: the *Guardian* and its editor had become serious news in both papers. It was even better journalism when MacGowan sued the *Guardian* chairman for slander. For three weeks, in a realization of a Fleet Street ideal, the *Guardian* became its own big news, with the chairman, the editor and the editor's journalistic style getting full-page treatment day after day. But MacGowan lost the case. And all Trinidad knew what until then had been known only to a few: that at the end of his contract MacGowan would be leaving.

MacGowan left. My father stayed behind. He became disturbed, fell ill, lost his job, and was idle and dependent for four years. In 1938, in the house of my mother's mother in Port of Spain, he came fully into my life for the first time. And in his clippings book, an old estate wages ledger, I came upon his relics of his heroic and hopeful time with MacGowan.

This was, very roughly, what I knew when, two years after I had written about Bogart and the life of the street, I thought of reconstructing the life of someone like my father. I had changed flats in London; and my mind went back to 1938, to my discovery of the few pieces of furniture which my father had brought with him to Port of Spain, the first furniture I had thought of as mine. I wanted to tell the story of the life as the story of the acquiring of those simple, precious pieces. The book took three years to write. It changed; and the writing changed me. I was writing about things I didn't know; and the book that came out was very much my father's book. It was written out of his journalism and stories, out of his knowledge, knowledge he had got from the way of looking MacGowan had trained him in. It was written out of his writing.

The book was read some years later—in Moscow—by a *New*

York Times writer, Israel Shenker. In 1970, in London, he interviewed me for his paper; he was doing a series on writers. Some weeks later he sent me a copy of a clipping from the *New York Herald Tribune* of 24 June 1933, and asked for my comments.

REPORTER SACRIFICES GOAT TO MOLLIFY HINDU GODDESS

Writer Kowtows to Kali to Escape Black Magic Death

Port of Spain, Trinidad, British West Indies. June 23 (CP). Threatened with death by the Hindu goddess Kali, Seepersad Naipaul, native writer, today offered a goat as sacrifice to appease the anger of the goddess.

Naipaul wrote newspaper articles revealing that native farmers of Hindu origin had defied government regulations for combating cattle diseases and had been substituting ancient rites of the goddess Kali to drive away the illness attacking their livestock.

The writer was told he would develop poisoning tomorrow, die on Sunday, and be buried on Monday unless he offered a goat sacrifice. Today he yielded to the entreaty of friends and relatives and made the demanded sacrifice.

I was staggered. I had no memory of this incident. I had read nothing about it in my father's ledger. I had heard nothing about it from my father or mother or anybody else. All that I remembered was that my father had a special horror of the Kali cult; and that he had told me once, with one of his rages about the family, that my mother's mother had been a devotee of Kali.

I wrote to Shenker that the story was probably one of MacGowan's joke stories, with my father trying to make himself his own news. That was what I believed, and the matter went to the back of my mind.

Two years later, when I was in Trinidad, I went to look at the *Guardian* file in the Port of Spain newspaper library. To me, until then, in spite of education, writing and travel, everything connected with my family past had seemed irrecoverable, existing only in fading memory. (All my father's documents, even his ledger, had been lost.)

Here were printed records. Here, in the sequence in which they had fallen in the mornings on the front steps of the Port of Spain house, were the *Guardian*s of 1938 and 1939, once looked at without being understood: the photographs of scholarship winners (such lucky men), the sports pages (with the same, often-used photographs of great cricketers), the cinema advertisements that had awakened such longing (Bobby Breen in *Rainbow on the River*).

And then, going back, I rediscovered parts of my father's ledger. I found that the ledger I had grown up with was not complete. My father had left out some things. The clipping Shenker had sent me told a true story. It was a bigger story than I had imagined, and it was not comic at all. It was the story of a great humiliation. It had occurred just when my father was winning through to a kind of independence, and had got started in his vocation. The independence was to go within months. The vocation—in a colonial Trinidad, without MacGowan—was to become meaningless; the vacancy was to be with my father for the rest of his life.

I had known about my father's long nervous illness. I hadn't know about its origins. My own ambitions had been seeded in something less than half knowledge of my father's early writing life.

6

MY FATHER, when I got to know him, was full of rages against my mother's family. But his early writings for the *Guardian* show that shortly after his marriage he was glamoured by the family.

They were a large brahmin family of landowners and pundits. Nearly all the sons-in-law were the sons of pundits, men with big names in our own private world, our island India. Caste had won my father admittance to the family, and for some time he seemed quite ready, in his *Guardian* reports, to act as a kind of family herald. "Popular Hindu Engagement—Chaguanas Link with Arouca": MacGowan couldn't have known, but this item of "Indian" news was really a family circular, court news: it was about the engagement of my grandmother's eldest granddaughter.

With the departure of my mother's father for India, and his subsequent death, the direction of the family had passed to the two eldest sons-in-law. They were brothers. They were ambitious and energetic men. They were concerned with the establishing of the local Hindu-Muslim school; with the affairs of the Local Road Board; and—in those days of the property franchise—with the higher politics connected with the island Legislative Council. They were also, as brahmins of the Tiwari clan, defenders of the orthodox Hindu faith—against Presbyterianism, then making converts among Hindus; and also against those reforming Hindu movements that had sent out missionaries from India. The brothers sought to be leaders; and they liked a fight. They were engaged in constant power games, which sometimes took a violent turn, with other families who also presumed to lead.

To belong to the family was to be in touch with much that was important in Indian life; or so my father made it. And in MacGowan's *Guardian* Indian news became mainly Chaguanas news, and Chaguanas news was often family news. "600 at Mass Meeting to Protest the Attitude of Cipriani." That was news, but it was also a family occasion: the meeting had been convened by the two senior sons-in-law. And when three days later the Chaguanas correspondent reported that feeling against Cipriani (a local politician) was still so strong that an eleven-year-old boy had been moved to speak "pathetically" at another public gathering, MacGowan couldn't have known that the boy in question was my mother's younger brother. (He became a Reader in mathematics at London University; and thirty years after his "pathetic" speech he also became the first leader of the opposition in independent Trinidad.)

My father might begin a political item like this: "At a surprise meeting last night . . ." And the chances were that the meeting had taken place in the "hall," the big downstairs room in the wooden house at the back of the main family house in Chaguanas.

But this closeness to the news-makers of Chaguanas had its strains. The family was a totalitarian organization. Decisions—about politics, about religious matters and, most importantly, about other families—were taken by a closed circle at the top—my grandmother and her two eldest sons-in-law. Everyone in the family was expected to fall into line; and most people did. There was something like a family propaganda machine constantly at work. It strengthened approved attitudes; it could also turn inwards, to discredit and humiliate dissidents. There was no plan; it simply happened like that, from the nature of our family organization. (When the two senior sons-in-law were eventually expelled from the family, the machine was easily turned against them.) And even today, when I meet descendants of families who were once "blacked" by my mother's family, I can feel I am in the presence of the enemy. To grow up in a family or clan like ours was to accept the ethos of the feud.

But what could be asked of a member of the family couldn't be asked of the reporter. The family had been strong supporters of the sitting member for the county in the Legislative Council. This man was a Hindu, and he was as good a legislator as the colonial constitution of the time permitted. Suddenly, perhaps for some Hindu sectarian reason, or because of a squabble over the running of the Hindu-Muslim school, our family decided to drop this man. They decided that at the next election, in 1933, they would support Mr. Robinson, who was a white man and the owner of large sugar estates in the area.

Mr. Robinson believed in child labour and his election speeches were invariably on this subject. He thought that any law that raised the school-leaving age to fourteen would be "inhuman." He was ready to be prosecuted "a thousand times," he was ready to go to jail, rather than stop giving work to the children of the poor. One of our family's ruling sons-in-law made a similar speech. Mr. Robinson, he said, was keeping young people out of jail.

It would not have been easy for my father, whose brother had gone to work as a child in the fields for eight cents a day, to be wholeheartedly on the family's side. But he tried; he gave a lot of attention to Mr. Robinson. Then my father had to report that the two sons-in-law had been charged with uttering menaces (allegedly, a "death threat") against someone on the other side.

Mr. Robinson lost the election. This was more than political news. This was a family defeat which, because it was at the hands of another Hindu family, was like a family humiliation; and my father had to report it in the jaunty *Guardian* style. The day after the election there was a riot in Chaguanas. A Robinson crowd of about a thousand attacked a bus carrying exultant supporters of the other side. The bus drove through the attacking crowd; a man in the crowd was killed; a man in the bus had his arm torn off; the police issued seventy summonses. That also had to be reported. And it would not have been at all easy for my father to report that—after another violent incident—the two senior sons-in-law of the family had appeared in court and had been fined. The family house was on the main road. Only a few hundred yards away, in a cluster, were the official buildings: the railway station, the warden's office, the police station and the court-house. The reporter would have had no trouble getting his story and returning, as it were, to base.

So my father's position in the family changed. From being the reporter who could act as family herald, he became the reporter who got people into the paper whether they wanted it or not; he became a man on the other side.

And, in fact, in one important way my father had always been on the other side. The family, with all its pundits, were defenders of the orthodox Hindu faith. My father wasn't. Later—just ten years later—when we were living in Port of Spain and our Hindu world was breaking up, my father was to write lyrically about Hindu rituals and Indian village life. But when he was a young man this Indian life was all he knew; it seemed stagnant and enduring; and he was critical. He was not alone. He belonged, or was sympathetic, to the reforming movement known as the Arya Samaj, which sought to make of Hinduism a pure philosophical faith. The Arya Samaj was against caste, pundits, animistic ritual. They were against child marriage; they were for the education of girls. On both these issues they clashed with the orthodox. And even smaller issues, in Trinidad, could lead to family feuds. What was the correct form of Hindu greeting? Could marriage ceremonies take place in daylight? Or did they, as the orthodox insisted, have to take place at night?

It was as reformer that my father had presented himself to MacGowan. And he had been encouraged by MacGowan: a "controversial" reporter was better for the paper, and MacGowan's attitude to Indians was one of paternal concern. And it was as a reformer that my father tackled the Indian side of the paralytic rabies story.

There had been a recrudescence of the disease in the weeks following the election, and Hindus were still not having their cattle vaccinated. One reason was that the government charge was too high—twenty-four cents a shot, at a time when a labourer earned thirty cents a day. But there was also a strong religious objection. And in some villages, as a charm against the disease, there was a ceremony of sacrifice to Kali, the black mother-goddess. Women went in procession through five villages, singing, and asking for alms for Kali. With the money they got they bought a goat. On the appointed day the goat was garlanded, its head cut off, and its blood sprinkled on the altar before the image of the goddess.

This was the story my father wrote, a descriptive piece, naming no names. But the reformer could not stay his hand: he spoke of "superstitious remedies" and "amazing superstitious practices," and that was how MacGowan played it up. Ten days later—what deliberations took place in those ten days?—my father received an anonymous threatening letter in Hindi. The letter said he was to perform the very ceremony he had criticised, or he was going to die in a week.

There is an indication, from my father's reporting of the incident, that the threat came from within the ruling circle of the family, perhaps from one of the senior sons-in-law. This man, at any rate, when approached, offered no help and seemed anxious only to confirm the contents of the letter. And, in the abasement that was demanded of my father, there is something that suggests family cruelty: as though the reporter, the errant family member, was to be punished this time for all his previous misdemeanours and disloyalties.

In the week that followed my father existed on three planes. He was the reporter who had become his own very big front-page story: "Next Sunday I am doomed to die." He was the reformer who wasn't going to yield to "ju-jus": "I won't sacrifice a goat." At the same time, as a man of feud-ridden Chaguanas, he was terrified of what he saw as a murder threat, and he was preparing to submit. Each role made nonsense of the other. And my father must have known it.

He wasn't going to sacrifice a goat to Kali. But then the readers of the *Guardian* discovered that he had made the sacrifice—not in Chaguanas, but in a little town a safe distance away.

A young English reporter, Sidney Rodin, who had been brought out recently by MacGowan to work on the *Guardian*, wrote the main story. It was a good piece of writing (and Rodin was to go back to London, to a long career in Fleet Street).

Rodin's report, full of emotion, catches all the details that must have horrified my father: the goat anointed and garlanded with hibiscus; red powder on its neck to symbolize its own blood, its own life; the cutlass on the tree stump; the flowers and fruit on the sacrificial altar.

My father, in Rodin's account, is, it might be said, a little to one side: a man who (unknown to Rodin) had been intended by his grandmother and mother to be a pundit, now for the first time going through priestly rites: a man in white, garlanded like the goat with hibiscus, offering sacrificial clove-scented fire to the image of the goddess, to the still living goat, to the onlookers, and then offering the severed goat's head on a brass plate.

My father, in his own report accompanying Rodin's story, has very little to say. He has no means of recording what he felt. He goes back to the reformist literature he had read; he plagiarizes some paragraphs. And he blusters. He will never sacrifice again, he says; he knows his faith now. And he records it as a little triumph that he didn't wear a loincloth: he went through the ceremony in trousers and shirt. The odd, illogical bluster continues the next day, on the front page of the Sunday paper. "Mr Naipaul Greets You!—No Poison Last Night." "Good morning, everybody! As you behold, Kali has not got me yet . . ."

It was his last piece of jauntiness from Chaguanas. Two months later he worked on a big hurricane story, but that was in the south of the island. His reports from Chaguanas became intermittent, and then he faded away from the paper.

A few months later MacGowan left Trinidad. There was an idea that my father might go with MacGowan to the United States; and he took out a passport. But my father didn't go. Dread of the unknown overcame him, as it had overcome him when he was a child, waiting on Nelson Island for the ship to take him to India. The passport remained crisp and unused in his desk, with his incomplete ledger.

He must have become unbalanced. It was no help when the

new editor of the *Guardian* took him off the staff and reduced him to a stringer. And soon he was quite ill.

I said to my mother one day when I came back from the Port of Spain newspaper library, "Why didn't you tell me about the sacrifice?"

She said, simply, "I didn't remember." She added, "Some things you will yourself to forget."

"What form did my father's madness take?"

"He looked in the mirror one day and couldn't see himself. And he began to scream."

The house where this terror befell him became unendurable to him. He left it. He became a wanderer, living in many different places, doing a variety of little jobs, dependent now on my mother's family, now on the family of his wealthy uncle by marriage. For thirteen years he had no house of his own.

My mother blamed MacGowan for the disaster. It gave her no pleasure to hear the name my father spoke so often or to follow MacGowan's later adventures. In 1942 we read in *Time* magazine that MacGowan, then nearly fifty, had gone as a war correspondent on the Dieppe raid and had written his story immediately afterwards, keeping himself awake (a MacGowan touch) on Benzedrine. And the *Guardian,* relenting towards its former editor, reported in 1944 that MacGowan had been taken prisoner by the Germans in France but had managed to escape, jumping off a train.

I understand my mother's attitude, but it isn't mine. It was no fault of MacGowan's that he had the bigger world to return to, and my father had only Trinidad. MacGowan transmitted his own idea of the journalist's or writer's vocation to my father. From no other source in colonial Trinidad could my father have got that. No other editor of the *Guardian* gave my father any sense of the worth of his calling. It was the idea of the vocation that exalted my father in the MacGowan days. It was in the day's story, and its reception by a sympathetic editor, that the day's struggle and the day's triumph lay. He wrote about Chaguanas, but the daily exercise of an admired craft would, in his own mind, have raised him above the constrictions of Chaguanas: he would have grown to feel protected by the word, and the quality of his calling. Then the props went. And he had only Chaguanas and Trinidad.

Admiration of the craft stayed with him. In 1936, in the middle of his illness—when I would have been staying in Chaguanas at my mother's family house—he sent me a little book, *The School of Poetry*, an anthology, really a decorated keepsake, edited by Alice Meynell. It had been marked down by the shop from forty-eight cents to twenty-four cents. It was his gift to his son of something noble, something connected with the word. Somehow the book survived all our moves. It is inscribed: "To Vidyadhar, from his father. Today you have reached the span of 3 years, 10 months and 15 days. And I make this present to you with this counsel in addition. Live up to the estate of man, follow truth, be kind and gentle and trust God."

Two years later, when my father got his *Guardian* job back, we moved to the house in Port of Spain. It was for me the serenest time of my childhood. I didn't know then how close my father was to his mental illness; and I didn't understand how much that job with the *Guardian* was for him a daily humiliation. He had had to plead for the job. In the desk were the many brusque replies, which I handled lovingly and often for the sake of the raised letter-heads.

Among the books in the bookcase were the books of comfort my father had picked up during his lost years: not only Marcus Aurelius and Epictetus, but also many mystical or quasi-religious books. One healing incantation from the time of his illness I got to know, because he taught it to me. It was a line he had adapted from Ella Wheeler Wilcox: "Even this shall pass away." It was an elastic consolation. It could deal with the pain of a moment, a day, life itself.

He never talked about the nature of his illness. And what is astonishing to me is that, with the vocation, he so accurately transmitted to me—without saying anything about it—his hysteria from the time when I didn't know him: his fear of extinction. That was his subsidiary gift to me. That fear became mine as well. It was linked with the idea of the vocation: the fear could be combated only by the exercise of the vocation.

And it was that fear, a panic about failing to be what I should be, rather than simple ambition, that was with me when I came down from Oxford in 1954 and began trying to write in London. My father had died the previous year. Our family was in distress. I should have done something for them, gone back to them. But, without having become a writer, I couldn't go back. In my eleventh month in London I wrote about Bogart. I wrote my book; I wrote another. I began to go back.

July–October 1982

Foreword to
The Adventures of Gurudeva

MY FATHER, Seepersad Naipaul, who was a journalist on the *Trinidad Guardian* for most of his working life, published a small collection of his short stories in Trinidad in 1943. He was thirty-seven; he had been a journalist off and on for fourteen years and had been writing stories for five. The booklet he put together, some seventy pages long, was called *Gurudeva and Other Indian Tales;* and it was my introduction to book-making. The printing was done, slowly, by the Guardian Commercial Printery; my father brought the proofs home bit by bit in his jacket pocket; and I shared his hysteria when the linotypists, falling into everyday ways, set—permanently, as it turned out—two of the stories in narrow newspaper-style columns.

The book, when it was published, drew one or two letters of abuse from people who thought that my father had written damagingly of our Indian community. There also came a letter many pages long, closely written in inks of different colours, the handwriting sloping this way and that, from a religion-crazed Muslim. This man later bought space in the *Trinidad Guardian* to print his photograph, with the query: *Who is this* [here he gave his name]*?* And so, at the age of eleven, with the publication of my father's book, I was given the beginnings of the main character of my own first novel.

Financially, the publication of *Gurudeva and Other Indian Tales* was a success. A thousand copies were printed and they sold at a dollar, four shillings, high for Trinidad in those days. But the copies went. Of the thousand copies—which at one time seemed so many, occupying so much space in a bedroom—only three or four now survive, in libraries; even my mother has no copy.

Shortly after the publication of *Gurudeva* my father left the *Guardian* for a government job that paid almost twice as well; and during the four or five years he worked for the government he wrote little for himself. He was, at first, "surveying" rural conditions for a government report. He was, therefore, surveying what he knew, his own background, the background of his early stories. But as a social surveyor compiling facts and figures and tables, no longer a writer concerned with the rituals and manners and what he had seen as the romantic essence of his community, my father was unsettled by what he saw. Out of this unsettlement, and with no thought of publication, he wrote a sketch, "In the Village," a personal response to the dereliction and despair by which we were surrounded and which we had all—even my father, in his early stories—taken for granted.

Later, out of a similar deep emotion, perhaps grief for his mother, who had died in great, Trinidad poverty in 1942, he wrote an autobiographical sketch. It was the only piece of autobiography my father permitted himself, if autobiography can be used of a story which more or less ends with the birth of the writer. But my father was obsessed by the circumstances of his birth and the cruelty of his father. I remember the passion that preceded the writing; I heard again and again the forty-year-old stories of meanness and of the expulsion of his pregnant mother from his father's house; and I remember taking down, at my father's dictation, a page or two of a version of this sketch.

A version: there were several versions of everything my father wrote. He always began to write suddenly, after a day or two of silence. He wrote very slowly; and there always came a moment when the emotion with which he had started seemed to have worked itself out and to my surprise—because I felt I had been landed with his emotion—something like literary mischief took over.

The autobiographical piece was read, long after it had been written, to a Port of Spain literary group which included Edgar Mittelholzer and, I believe, the young George Lamming. There was objection to the biblical language and especially to the use of "ere" for "before"; but my father ignored the objection and I, who was very much under the spell of the story, supported him. "In the Village" was printed in a Jamaican magazine edited by Philip Sherlock.

A reading to a small group, publication in a magazine soon lost to view: writing in Trinidad was an amateur activity, and this was all the encouragement a writer could expect. There were no magazines that paid; there were no established magazines; there was only the *Guardian*. A writer like Alfred Mendes, who in the 1930s had had two novels published by Duckworth in London (one with an introduction by Aldous Huxley and a blurb by Anthony Powell), was said to get as much as twenty dollars, four guineas, for a story in the *Guardian* Sunday supplement; my father only got five dollars, a guinea. My father was a purely local writer, and writers like that ran the risk of ridicule; one of the criticisms of my father's book that I heard at school was that it had been done only for the money.

But attitudes were soon to change. In 1949, the Hogarth Press published Edgar Mittelholzer's novel, *A Morning at the Office;* Mittelholzer had for some time been regarded as another local writer. And then there at last appeared a market. Henry Swanzy was editing *Caribbean Voices* for the BBC Caribbean Service. He had standards and enthusiasm. He took local writing seriously and lifted it above the local. And the BBC paid; not quite at their celebrated guinea-a-minute rate, but sufficiently well—fifty dollars a story, sixty dollars, eighty dollars—to spread a new idea of the value of writing.

Henry Swanzy used two of my father's early stories on *Caribbean Voices*. And from 1950, when he left the government to go back to the *Guardian*, to 1953, when he died, it was for *Caribbean Voices* that my father wrote. In these three years, in circumstances deteriorating month by month—the low *Guardian* pay, debt, a heart attack and subsequent physical incapacity, the hopeless, wounded longing to publish a real book and become in his own eyes a writer—in these three years, with the stimulus of that weekly radio programme from London, my father, I believe, found his voice as a writer, developed his own comic gift, and wrote his best stories.

I didn't participate in the writing of these stories: I didn't watch them grow, or give advice, as I had done with the others. In 1949 I had won a Trinidad government scholarship, and in 1950 I left home to come to England to take up the scholarship. I left my father at the beginning of a story called "The Engagement"; and it was two years before I read the finished story.

My father wrote me once and sometimes twice a week. His letters, like mine to him, were mainly about money and writing. When Henry Swanzy, in his half-yearly review of *Caribbean Voices*, praised "The Engagement," my father, who had never been praised like that before, wrote me: "I am beginning to feel I *could* have been a writer." But we both felt ourselves in our different ways stalled, he almost at the end of his life, I at the beginning of mine; and our correspondence, as time went on, as he became more broken, and I became more separate from him and Trinidad, more adrift in England, became one of half-despairing mutual encouragement. I had sent him some books by R. K. Narayan, the Indian writer. In March 1952 he wrote: "You were right about R. K. Narayan. I like his short stories . . . he seems gifted and has made a go of his talent, which in my own case I haven't even spotted."

In that month he sent me two versions of a story called "My Uncle Dalloo." He was uncertain about this story, which he thought long-winded, and wanted me to send what I thought was the better version to Henry Swanzy. I like the story now, for its detail and the drama of its detail; in a small space it creates and peoples a landscape, and the vision is personal. My father hadn't done anything like that before, anything with that amount of historical detail, and I can see the care with which the story is written. I can imagine how those details which he was worried about, and yet was unwilling to lose, were worked over. But at the time—I was nineteen—I took the quality of the vision for granted and saw only the incompleteness of the narrative: my father, working in isolation, had, it might be said, outgrown me.

Henry Swanzy didn't use "My Uncle Dalloo." But his judgement of my father's later work was sounder than mine, and he used nearly everything else my father sent him. In June 1953, four months before my father died, Henry Swanzy, at my father's request, asked me to read "Ramdas and the Cow" for *Caribbean Voices*. The reading fee was four guineas. With the money I bought the Parker pen which I still have and with which I am writing this foreword.

2

NAIPAUL (or Naipal or Nypal, in earlier transliterations: the transliteration of Hindi names can seldom be exact) was the name of my father's father; birth certificates and other legal requirements have now made it our family name. He was brought to Trinidad as a baby from eastern Uttar Pradesh at some time in the 1880s, as I work it out.

He received no English education but, in the immemorial Hindu way, as though Trinidad were India, he was sent—as a brahmin boy of the Panday clan (or the Parray clan: again, the transliteration is difficult)—to the house of a brahmin to be trained as a pundit. This was what he became; he also, as I have heard, became a small dealer in those things needed for Hindu rituals. He married and had three children; but he died when he was still quite young and his family, unprotected, was soon destitute. My father once told me that at times there wasn't oil for a lamp.

There was some talk, among other branches of the family, of sending the mother and the children back to India; but that plan fell through, and the dependent family was scattered among various relations. My father's elder brother, still only a child, was sent out to work in the fields at fourpence a day; but it was decided that my father, as the youngest of the children, should be educated and perhaps made a pundit, like his father. And that family fracture shows to this day in their descendants. My father's brother, by immense labour, became a small cane-farmer. When I went to see him in 1972, not long before he died, I found him enraged, crying for his childhood and that fourpence a day. My father's sister made two unhappy marriages; she remained, as it were, dazed by Trinidad; until her death in 1972—more cheerful than her brother, though in a house not her own—she spoke only Hindi and could hardly understand English.

My father received an elementary-school education; he learned English and Hindi. But the attempt to make him a pundit failed. Instead, he began doing odd jobs, attached to the household of a relative (later a millionaire) in that very village of El Dorado which he was to survey more than twenty years later for the government and write about in "In the Village."

I do not know how, in such a setting, in those circumstances of dependence and uncertainty, and with no example, the wish to be a writer came to my father. But I feel now, reading the stories after a long time and seeing so clearly (what was once hidden from me) the brahmin standpoint from which they are written, that it might have been the caste-sense, the Hindu reverence for learning and the word, awakened by the beginnings of an English education and a Hindu religious training. In one letter to me he seems to say that he was trying to write when he was fourteen.

He was concerned from the start with Hinduism and the practices of Hinduism. His acquaintance with pundits had given him something of the puritan brahmin prejudice against pundits, professional priests, stage-managers of ritual, as "tradesmen." But he had also been given some knowledge of Hindu thought, which he valued; and on this knowledge, evident in the stories, he continued to build throughout his life; as late as 1951 he was writing me ecstatically about Aurobindo's commentaries on the Gita.

The Indian immigrants in Trinidad, and especially the Hindus among them, belonged in the main to the peasantry of the Gangetic plain. They were part of an old and perhaps an ancient India. (It was entrancing to me, when I read Fustel de Coulange's *The Ancient City,* to discover that many of the customs, which with us in Trinidad, even in my childhood, were still like instincts, had survived from the pre-classical world.) This peasantry, transported to Trinidad, hadn't been touched by the great Indian reform movements of the nineteenth century. Reform became an issue only with the arrival of reformist missionaries from India in the 1920s, at a time when in India itself religious reform was merging into political rebellion.

In the great and sometimes violent debates that followed in Trinidad—debates that remained unknown outside the Indian community and are today forgotten by everybody—my father was on the side of reform. The broad satire of the latter part of *Gurudeva*—written in the last year of his life, but not sent to Henry Swanzy—shouldn't be misinterpreted: there my father fights the old battles again, with the passion that in the 1930s had made him spend scarce money on a satirical reform pamphlet, *Religion and the Trinidad East Indians,* one of the books of my childhood, but now lost.

It was on Indian or Hindu topics that my father began writing for the *Trinidad Guardian*, in 1929. The paper had a new editor, Gault MacGowan. He had come from *The Times* and in Trinidad was like a man unleashed. The *Trinidad Guardian*, before MacGowan, was a half-dead colonial newspaper: a large border of advertisements on its front page, a small central patch of closely printed cables. MacGowan's brief was to modernize the *Guardian*. He scrapped that front page. But his taste for drama went beyond the typographical and he began to unsettle some people. Voodoo in backyards, obeah, prisoners escaping from Devil's Island, vampire bats: when the editor of the rival *Port of Spain Gazette* said that MacGowan was killing the tourist trade, MacGowan sued and won. But MacGowan was more than a sensationalist. He was new to Trinidad, discovering Trinidad, and he took nothing for granted. He saw stories everywhere; he could make stories out of nothing; his paper was like a daily celebration of the varied life of the island. But sometimes his wit could run away with him; and the end came when he became involved in a lawsuit with his own employers (which the *Trinidad Guardian*, MacGowan still the editor, reported at length, day after day, so that, in a perfection of the kind of journalism his employers were objecting to, the paper became its own news).

My father had written to MacGowan; and MacGowan, who had been to India and was interested in Indian matters, thought that my father should be encouraged. My father's iconoclastic views, and their journalistic possibilities, must have appealed to him. He became my father's teacher—beginning no doubt with English which, it must be remembered, was for my father an acquired language—and my father never lost his admiration and affection for the man who, as he often said, had taught him how to write. More than twenty years later, in 1951, my father wrote me: "And as to a writer being hated or liked—I think it's the other way to what you think: a man is doing his work well when people begin *liking* him. I have never forgotten what Gault MacGowan told me years ago: 'Write sympathetically';

and this, I suppose, in no way prevents us from writing truthfully, even brightly."

My father began on the *Guardian* as the freelance contributor of a "controversial" weekly column. The column—in which I think MacGowan's improving hand can often be detected—was, provocatively, signed "The Pundit"; and my father remembered the Pundit's words well enough to give blocks of them, years later, to Mr. Sohun, the Presbyterian Indian schoolmaster, in the latter part of *Gurudeva. Gurudeva* has other echoes of my father's early journalism: Gurudeva's beating up of the drunken old stick-fighter must, I feel, have its origin in the news story my father, now a regular country correspondent for the *Guardian,* wrote in 1930: "Fight Challenge Accepted—Jerningham Junction 'Bully' Badly Injured—Six Men Arrested." A country brawl dramatized, the personalities brought close to the reader, made more than names in a court report: this was MacGowan's style, and it became my father's.

It was through his journalism on MacGowan's *Guardian* that my father arrived at that vision of the countryside and its people which he later transferred to his stories. And the stories have something of the integrity of the journalism: they are written from within a community and seem to be addressed to that community: a Hindu community essentially, which, because the writer sees it as whole, he can at times make romantic and at other times satirize. There is reformist passion; but even when there is shock there is nothing of the protest—common in early colonial writing—that implies an outside audience; the barbs are all turned inwards. This is part of the distinctiveness of the stories. I stress it because this way of looking, from being my father's, became mine: my father's early stories created my background for me.

But it was a partial vision. A story called "Panchayat," about a family quarrel, reads like a pastoral romance: the people in that story exist completely within a Hindu culture and recognize no other. The wronged wife does not take her husband to the alien law courts; she calls a panchayat against him. The respected village elders assemble; the wife and the husband state their cases without rancour; everyone is wise and dignified and acknowledges *dharma*, the Hindu right way, the way of piety, the old way. But Trinidad, and not India, is in the background. These people have been transported; old ways and old allegiances are being eroded fast. The setting, which is not described because it is taken for granted, is one of big estates, workers' barracks, huts. It is like the setting of "In the Village"; but that vision of material and cultural dereliction comes later, and it is some time before it can be accommodated in the stories.

Romance simplified; but it was a way of looking. And it was more than a seeking out of the picturesque; it was also, as I have since grown to understand, a way of concealing personal pain. My father once wrote me: "I have hardly written a story in which the principal characters have not been members of my own family." And the wronged wife of "Panchayat"—as I understood only the other day—was really my father's sister; the details in that story are all true. Her marriage to a Punjabi brahmin (a learned man, who could read Persian, as she told me with pride on her deathbed) was a disaster. My father suffered for her. In the story ritual blurs the pain and, fittingly, all ends well; in life the disaster continued. My father hated his father for his cruelty and meanness; yet when, in his autobiographical sketch, he came to write about his father, he wrote a tale of pure romance, in which again old ritual, lovingly described, can only lead to reconciliation. And my father, in spite of my encouragement, could never take that story any further.

He often spoke of doing an autobiographical novel. Sometimes he said it would be easy; but once he wrote that parts of it would be difficult; he would have trouble selecting the incidents. When in 1952 he sent me "My Uncle Dalloo"—which he described in another letter, apologetically, as a sketch—he wrote: "I'd like you to read it carefully, and if you think it good enough, send it to Mr Swanzy, with a note that it's from me; and that it is part of a chapter of a novel I'm doing. Indeed, this is what I aim to do with it. As soon as you can, get working on a novel. Write of things as they are happening now, be realistic, humorous when this comes in pat, but don't make it deliberately so. If you are at a loss for a theme, take me for it. Begin: 'He sat before the little table writing down the animal counterparts of all his wife's family. He was very analytical about it. He wanted to be correct; went to work like a scientist. He wrote, "The She-Fox," then "The Scorpion"; at the end of five minutes he produced a list which read as follows: ...' All this is just a jest, but you can really do it."

But for him it wasn't a jest. Once romance and its simplifications had been left behind, these little impulses of caricature (no more than impulses, and sometimes written out in letters to me), the opposite of MacGowan's "Write sympathetically," were all he could manage when he came to consider himself and the course of his life. He wrote up the animal-counterparts episode himself (I am sure he was writing it when he wrote that letter to me) and made it part of *Gurudeva,* which had become his fictional hold-all. But even there the episode is sudden and out of character. There is something unresolved about it; the passion is raw and comes out, damagingly, as a piece of gratuitous cruelty on the part of the writer. My father was unhappy about the episode; but he could do no more with it. And this was in the last year of his life, when as a writer—but only looking away from himself—he could acknowledge some of the pain about his family he had once tried to hide, and was able to blend romance and the later vision of dereliction into a purer kind of comedy.

It is my father's sister—once the wronged wife of "Panchayat," a figure of sorrow in a classical Hindu tableau—who ten years afterwards appears as a road-mender's wife in another story and acts as a kind of comic chorus: the road-mender was the man of lesser caste with whom she went to live after she had separated from her first husband, the Punjabi brahmin. Ramdas of "Ramdas and the Cow"—the Hindu tormented by the possession of a sixty-dollar cow which turns out to be barren—is my father's elder brother in middle age.

The comedy was for others. My father remained unwilling to look at his own life. All that material, which might have committed him to longer work and a longer view, remained locked up and unused. Certain things can never become material. My father never in his life reached that point of rest from which he could look back at his past. His last years, when he found his voice as a writer, were years of especial distress and anxiety; he was part of the dereliction he wrote about.

My father's elder brother, at the end of his life, was enraged, as I have said. This sturdy old man, whose life might have been judged a success, was broken by memories of his childhood; self-knowledge had come to him late. My father's own crisis had come at an earlier age; it had been hastened by his journalism. One day in 1934, when he was twenty-eight, five years after he had been writing for the *Guardian,* and some months after Gault MacGowan had left the paper and Trinidad, my father looked in the mirror and thought he couldn't see himself. It was the beginning of a long mental illness that caused him for a time to be unemployed, and as dependent as he had been in his childhood. It was after his recovery that he began writing stories and set himself the goal of the book.

3

SHORTLY BEFORE he died, in 1953, my father assembled all the stories he wanted to keep and sent them to me. He wanted me to get them published as a book. Publication for him, the real book, meant publication in London. But I did not think the stories publishable outside Trinidad, and I did nothing about them.

The stories, especially the early ones, in which I felt I had participated, never ceased to be important to me. But as the years passed—and although I cannibalized his autobiographical sketch for the beginning of one of my own books—my attachment to the stories became sentimental. I valued them less for what they were (or the memory of what they were) than for what, long before, they had given me: a way of looking, an example of labour, a knowledge of the literary process, a sense of the order and special reality (at once simpler and sharper than life) that written words could be seen to create. I thought of them, as I thought of my father's letters, as a private possession.

But the memory of my father's 1943 booklet, *Gurudeva and Other Indian Tales,* has never altogether died in Trinidad. Twelve years after his death, my father's stories were remembered by Henry Swanzy in a *New Statesman* issue on Commonwealth writing. In Trinidad itself the attitude to local writing has changed. And my own view has grown longer. I no longer look in the stories for what isn't there; and I see them now as a valuable part of the literature of the region.

They are a unique record of the life of the Indian or Hindu community in Trinidad in the first fifty years of the century. They move from a comprehension of the old India in which the community is at first embedded to an understanding of the colonial Trinidad which defines itself as their background, into which they then emerge. To write about a community which has not been written about is not easy. To write about this community was especially difficult; it required unusual knowledge and an unusual breadth of sympathy.

And the writer himself was part of the process of change. This wasn't always clear to me. But I find it remarkable now that a writer, beginning in the old Hindu world, one isolated segment of it, where all the answers had been given and the rituals perfected, and where, apart from religious texts, the only writings known were the old epics of the *Ramayana* and the *Mahabharat;* leaving that to enter a new world and a new language; using simple, easily detectable models—Pearl Buck, O. Henry; I find it remarkable that such a writer, working always in isolation, should have gone so far. I don't think my father read Gogol; but these stories, at their best, have something of the quality of the Ukrainian stories Gogol wrote when he was a very young man. There is the same eye that lingers lovingly over what might at first seem nondescript. Landscape, dwellings, people: there is the same assembling of sharp detail. The drama lies in that; when what has been relished is recorded and fixed, the story is over.

Gogol at the beginning of his writing life, my father at the end of his: even if the comparison is just, it can mislead. After his young man's comedy and satire, after the discovery and exercise of his talent, Gogol had Russia to fall back on and claim. It was the other way with my father. From a vision of a whole Hindu society he moved, through reformist passion, which was an expression of his brahmin confidence, to a vision of disorder and destitution, of which he discovered himself to be part. At the end he had nothing to claim; it was out of this that he created comedy.

The process is illustrated by *Gurudeva*. This story isn't satisfactory, especially in some of its later sections; and my father knew it. Part of the trouble is that the story was written in two stages. The early sections, which were written in 1941–2, tell of the beginnings of a village strongman. The character (based, remotely, on someone who had married into my mother's family but had then been expelled from it, the mention of his name forbidden) is not as negligible as he might appear now. He belongs to the early 1930s and, in those days of restricted franchise, he might have developed (as the original threatened to develop) into a district politician. Although in the story he is simplified, and his idea of manhood ridiculed as thuggery and a perversion of the caste instinct, Gurudeva is felt to be a figure. And in its selection of strong, brief incidents, its gradual peopling of an apparently self-contained Indian countryside (other communities are far away), this part of the story is like the beginning of a rural epic.

Ten years later, when my father returned to the story (and brought Gurudeva back from jail, where in 1942 he had sent him), the epic tone couldn't be sustained. Gurudeva's Indian world was not as stable as Gurudeva, or the writer, thought. The society had been undermined; its values had to compete with other values; the world outside the village could no longer be denied. As seen in 1950–2, Gurudeva, the caste bully of the 1930s, becomes an easy target. Too easy: the irony and awe with which he had been handled in the first part of the story turn to broad satire, and the satire defeats itself.

Mr. Sohun the schoolmaster, the Presbyterian convert, holds himself up, and is held up by the writer, as a rational man, freed from Hindu prejudice and obscurantism. But Mr. Sohun, whose words in the 1930s might have seemed wise, is himself now seen more clearly. It is hinted—he hints himself: my father makes him talk too much—that he is of low caste. His Presbyterianism is more than an escape from this: it is, as Gurudeva says with sly compassion, Mr. Sohun's bread and butter, a condition of his employment as a teacher in the Canadian Mission school. Mr. Sohun's son has the un-Indian name of Ellway. But the boy so defiantly named doesn't seem to have done much or to have much to do. When Gurudeva calls, Ellway is at home, noisily knocking up fowl-coops: the detail sticks out.

In fact, the erosion of the old society has exposed Mr. Sohun, and the writer, as much as Gurudeva. The writer senses this; his attitude to Gurudeva changes. The story jumps from the 1930s to the late 1940s. Gurudeva, no longer a caste bully and a threat, becomes a figure of comedy; and, curiously, his stature grows. He is written into the story of "Ramdas and the Cow" (originally an independent story); turning satirist himself, he writes down the animal counterparts of his wife's family and begins to approximate to his creator; at the end, abandoned by wife and girlfriend and left alone, he is a kind of brahmin, an upholder of what remains of old values, but powerless. He has travelled the way of his baffled creator.

Writers need a source of strength other than that which they find in their talent. Literary talent doesn't exist by itself; it feeds on a society and depends for its development on the nature of that society. What is true of my father is true of other writers of the region. The writer begins with his talent, finds confidence in his talent, but then discovers that it isn't enough, that, in a society as deformed as ours, by the exercise of his talent he has set himself adrift.

4

I HAVE NOT attempted to change the idiosyncrasies of my father's English; I have corrected only one or two obvious errors. In the later stories (partly because he was writing for the radio) he wrote phonetic dialogue. Phonetic dialogue—apart from its inevitable absurdities: *eggszactly* for "exactly," *w'at* for "what"—falsifies the pace of speech, sets up false associations, is meaningless to people who don't know the idiom and unnecessary to those who do. The rhythm of broken language is sufficiently indicated by the construction of a sentence. I have toned down this phonetic dialogue, modelling myself on my father's more instinctive and subtle rendering of speech in *Gurudeva and Other Indian Tales;* like my father in that early booklet, I have not aimed at uniformity.

My father dedicated his stories to me. But the style of publication has changed; and I would like to extend this dedication to the two men who stand at the beginning and end of my father's writing career: to Gault MacGowan, to whom I know my father wanted to dedicate *Gurudeva and Other Indian Tales* in 1943; and to Henry Swanzy.

June 1975

Foreword to
A House for Mr. Biswas

(Knopf, 1983)

OF ALL MY BOOKS this is the one that is closest to me. It is the most personal, created out of what I saw and felt as a child. It also contains, I believe, some of my funniest writing. I began as a comic writer and still consider myself one. In middle age now, I have no higher literary ambition than to write a piece of comedy that might complement or match this early book.

The book took three years to write. It felt like a career; and there was a short period, towards the end of the writing, when I do believe I knew all or much of the book by heart. The labour ended; the book began to recede. And I found that I was unwilling to re-enter the world I had created, unwilling to expose myself again to the emotions that lay below the comedy. I became nervous of the book. I haven't read it since I passed the proofs in May 1961.

My first direct contact with the book since the proof-reading came two years ago, in 1981. I was in Cyprus, in the house of a friend. Late one evening the radio was turned on, to the BBC World Service. I was expecting a news bulletin. Instead, an instalment of my book was announced. The previous year the book had been serialized on the BBC in England as "A Book at Bedtime." The serialization was now being repeated on the World Service. I listened. And in no time, though the instalment was comic, though the book had inevitably been much abridged, and the linking words were not always mine, I was in tears, swamped by the emotions I had tried to shield myself from for twenty years. *Lacrimae rerum*, "the tears of things," the tears in things: to the feeling for the things written about—the passions and nerves of my early life—there was added a feeling for the time of the writing—the ambition, the tenacity, the innocence. My literary ambition had grown out of my early life; the two were intertwined; the tears were for a double innocence.

When I was eleven, in 1943, in Trinidad, in a setting and family circumstances like those described in this book, I decided to be a writer. The ambition was given me by my father. In Trinidad, a small agricultural colony, where nearly everyone was poor and most people were uneducated, he had made himself into a journalist. At a certain stage—not for money or fame (there was no local market), but out of some private need—he had begun to write short stories. Not formally educated, a nibbler of books rather than a reader, my father worshipped writing and writers. He made the vocation of the writer seem the noblest in the world; and I decided to be that noble thing.

I had no gift. At least, I was aware of none. I had no precocious way with words, no talent for fantasy or story-telling. But I began to build my life around the writing ambition. The gift, I thought, was going to come later, when I grew up. Purely from wishing to be a writer, I thought of myself as a writer. Since the age of sixteen or so I don't believe a day has passed without my contemplating in some way this fact about myself. There were one or two boys at Queen's Royal College in Trinidad who wrote better than I. There was at least one boy (he committed suicide shortly after leaving school) who was far better read and had a more elegant mind. The literary superiority of this boy didn't make me doubt my vocation. I just thought it odd—after all, it was I who was going to be the writer.

In 1948, when I was sixteen, I won a Trinidad government scholarship. This scholarship could have taken me to any university or institute of higher education in the British Commonwealth and given me any profession. I decided to go to Oxford and do a simple degree in English. I went in 1950. Really, I went to Oxford in order at last to write. Or more correctly, to allow writing to come to me. I had always thought that the writing gift would come to me of itself as a kind of illumination and blessing, a fair reward for the long ambition. It didn't come. My efforts, when I made them, were forced, unfelt. I didn't see how I could ever write a book. I was, of course, too young to write: hardly with adult judgement, and too close to childhood to see the completeness and value of that experience. But I couldn't know that at the time. And in my solitude in England, doubting my vocation and myself, I drifted into something like a mental illness. This lasted for much of my time at Oxford. Just when that depression was beginning to lift, my father died in Trinidad.

In Trinidad, as a child, I had been supported by the idea of the literary life that awaited me when I grew up. It had been a prospect of romance. I was in a state of psychological destitution when—having no money, besides—I went to London after leaving Oxford in 1954, to make my way as a writer. Thirty years later, I can easily make present to myself again the anxiety of that time: to have found no talent, to have written no book, to be null and unprotected in the busy world. It is that anxiety— the fear of destitution in all its forms, the vision of the abyss— that lies below the comedy of the present book.

A book with emotions so close to me did not immediately come. It came after I had spent three years in London and written three works of fiction. It had been necessary for me to develop some skill, and through practice to begin to see myself and get an idea of the nature of my talent. I had had an intimation—just an intimation, nothing formulated—that the years of ambition and thinking of myself as a writer had in fact prepared me for writing. I had been a looker; I had trained my memory and developed a faculty of recall.

Just as, because I was to be a writer, I had as a child fallen into the habit (though not at school) of speaking very fast and then immediately silently mouthing the words I had spoken, to check them, so I automatically—thinking of it as a newsreel—mentally replayed every meeting or adventure, to check and assess the meaning and purpose of people's words. I had done no writing as a child, had told no stories; but I had trained myself to an acute feeling for human character as expressed in words and faces, gestures and the shape of bodies. I had thought, when I began to write in London, that my life was a blank. Through the act of writing, and the need always to write more, I discovered I had processed and stored a great deal.

So the idea for this big book came to me when I was ready for it. The original idea was simple, even formal: to tell the story of a man like my father, and, for the sake of narrative shape, to tell the story of the life as the story of the acquiring of the simple possessions by which the man is surrounded at his death. In the writing the book changed. It became the story of a man's search for a house and all that the possession of one's own house implies. The first idea—personal, lodged in me since childhood, but also perhaps reinforced by an all but erased memory of a D. H. Lawrence story called "Things"—wasn't false. But it was too formal for a novel. The second idea, about the house, was larger, better. It also contained more of the truth. The novel, once it had ceased to be an idea and had begun to exist as a novel, called up its own truth.

For me to write the story of a man like my father was, in the beginning at any rate, to attempt pure fiction, if only because I was writing of things before my time. The transplanted Hindu-Muslim rural culture of Trinidad into which my father was born early in the century was still a whole culture, close to India. When I was of an age to observe, that culture had begun to weaken; and the time of wholeness had seemed to me as far away as India itself, and almost dateless. I knew little about the Trinidad Indian village way of life. I was a town boy; I had grown up in Port of Spain. I had memories of my father's conversation; I also had his short stories. These stories, not many, were mainly about old rituals. They were my father's own way of looking back, in his unhappy thirties and forties. This was what my fantasy had to work on.

So the present novel begins with events twice removed, in an antique, "pastoral" time, and almost in a land of the imagination. The real world gradually defines itself, but it is still for the writer an imagined world. The novel is well established, its tone set, when my own wide-awake memories take over. So the book is a work of the imagination. It is obviously not "made up," created out of nothing. But it does not tell a literal truth. The pattern in the narrative of widening vision and a widening world, though I believe it to be historically true of the people concerned, derives also from the child's way of experiencing. It was on the partial knowledge of a child—myself—and his intuitions and emotion that the writer's imagination went to work. There is more fantasy, and emotion, in this novel than in my later novels, where the intelligence is more in command.

The novel took some time to get going. I began it, or began writing towards it, in the latter half of 1957. I was living on the draughty attic floor of a big Edwardian house in Muswell Hill in north London. The sitting room was choked with my landlady's unwanted furniture. The furniture was from her first marriage; she had lived in Malaya before the war, had seen or glimpsed Somerset Maugham out there, and she told me, as though letting me into a secret, that he was "a nasty little man." When middle-class Muswell Hill dinner parties were given downstairs (with the help of a very old uniformed maid, a relic, like her mistress, of a dead age), there was the modest smell of Dutch cigars. Upstairs, in my attic, the tattered old sitting-room carpet, its colours faded with old dust, rippled in the winter gales. There was also a mouse somewhere in the room.

Old furniture, "things," homelessness: they were more than ideas when I began writing. I had just, after ten weeks, left a well-paid but pointless and enervating job (my first and only full-time job). So, from having money, I had none again. I was also trying to do reviews for the *New Statesman*, which in 1957 was near the peak of its reputation. The *New Statesman* tormented me more than the novel. I was trying too hard with the trial reviews, and making myself clouded and physically queasy day after day. But the *New Statesman* gave me more than one chance; and at last, quite suddenly one day, I found my reviewer's voice. Two or three months later the novel came alive; as with the reviewing; it seemed to happen at a particular moment. Soon the excitement of the novel displaced the glamour of the *New Statesman*. And then for two years I wrote in perfect conditions.

I left Muswell Hill and the attic flat and moved south of the river to Streatham Hill. For twenty-five pounds a month I had the whole of the upper floor of a semi-detached house, with my own entrance off the tiled downstairs hall. My landlady's daughter lived alone downstairs; and she did a job all day. I had more than changed flats: for the first time in my life I enjoyed solitude and freedom in a house. And just as, in the novel, I was able to let myself go, so in the solitude of the quiet, friendly house in Streatham Hill I could let myself go. There is a storm scene in the book, with black, biting ants. It was written (perhaps in its second draft) with the curtains drawn, and by candlelight. I wanted the atmosphere, and wanted to remind myself of the moving shadows thrown by the oil-lamps of part of my childhood.

My landlady's daughter read a lot and was a great buyer of books. I don't believe she cared for those I had published, but during all my time in her house I felt her as an understanding, encouraging presence, never obtrusive. She made me a gift one day of a little square wool rug she had made herself. It was some weeks before, turning the square rug another way, I saw that the pattern was not abstract, but made up of my initials. She subscribed to the *New Statesman;* and it was for her, as much as for the literary editor of the *New Statesman*, that every four weeks I wrote my review of novels.

In that week I also did other journalism, mainly radio talks for the BBC Overseas Service. Then for three weeks at a stretch

I worked on the novel. I wrote with joy. And as I wrote, my conviction grew. My childhood dream of writing had been a dream of fame and escape and an imagined elegant style of life. Nothing in my father's example or conversation had prepared me for the difficulties of narrative prose, of finding a voice, the difficulties of going on to the next book and the next, the searching of oneself for matter to write about. But, equally, nothing had prepared me for the liberation and absorption of this extended literary labour, the joy of allowing fantasy to play on stored experience, the joy of the comedy that so naturally offered itself, the joy of language. The right words seemed to dance above my head; I plucked them down at will. I took chances with language. Before this, out of my beginner's caution, I had been strict with myself.

In the last year mental and physical fatigue touched me. I had never before experienced that depth of fatigue. I became aware of how much I had given to the book, and I thought that I could never be adequately rewarded for the labour. And I believe it is true to say that the labour had burnt up thoughts of reward. Often, out in the Streatham Hill streets, momentarily away from the book, shopping perhaps, I thought: "If someone were to offer me a million pounds on condition that I leave the book unfinished, I would turn the money down." Though I didn't really need one, I bought a new typewriter to type out the precious finished manuscript. But I was too tired to type to the end; that had to be done professionally.

When the book was handed in, I went abroad for seven months. An opportunity for travel in the Caribbean and South America had been given me by the Trinidad government. Colonial Trinidad had sent me to Oxford in 1950, and I had made myself a writer. Self-governing Trinidad sent me on a colonial tour in 1960, and by this accident I became a traveller. It wasn't absolutely the end of the Streatham Hill house—I was to go back there for nine months, to write a book about my travels. But that was another kind of writing, another skill. It could be as taxing as fiction; it demanded in some ways an equivalent completeness of man and writer. But it engaged another part of the brain. No play of fantasy was required; the writer would never regard with wonder what he had drawn out of himself, the unsuspected truths turned up by the imagination.

The two years spent on this novel in Streatham Hill remain the most consuming, the most fulfilled, the happiest years of my life. They were my Eden. Hence, more than twenty years later, the tears in Cyprus.

March 1983

PART TWO

Indian Autobiographies

THE DERELICTION of India overwhelms the visitor; and it seems reasonable to imagine that the Indian who leaves his country, and all its assumptions, for the first time is likely to be unsettled. But in Indian autobiographies* there is no hint of unsettlement: people are their designations and functions, and places little more than their names. "We reached Southampton, as far as I can remember, on a Saturday." This is Gandhi writing in 1925 of his arrival in England as a student in 1889. That it was a Saturday was more important to him than that he had exchanged Bombay for Southampton. He had landed in a white flannel suit and couldn't get at his luggage until Monday. So Southampton is no more than an experience of embarrassment and is never described; as later London, never described, is converted into a series of small spiritual experiences, the vows of vegetarianism and chastity being more important than the city of the 1890s. A place is its name.

---

*The Story of My Experiments with Truth, by M. K. Gandhi, translated by Mahadev Desai, 1966.
Punjabi Century, by Prakash Lal Tandon, 1963.
My Public Life, by Mirza Ismail, 1954.
A Passage to England, by Nirad Chaudhuri, 1959.
The Autobiography of an Unknown Indian, by Nirad Chaudhuri, 1951.

London was just too big for me and the two days I spent there so overwhelming that I was glad to leave for Manchester. My brother had arranged some digs in advance so that I settled in straight away.

We are forty years beyond Gandhi, but the tone in *Punjabi Century,* the memoirs of a high business executive, remains the same. India is one place, England another. There can be no contrast, no shock in reverse. It is only near the end of *My Public Life* that Sir Mirza Ismail, after listing the recommendations he made to President Sukarno for the improvement of the Indonesian administration—he recommended four new colleges, five new stadiums and "publication of the President's speeches in book form"—it is only after this that he observes:

> The standard of living is higher in Indonesia than in India. People are better clad and better fed, although cloth is much dearer. One hardly sees the miserable specimens of humanity that one comes across in the big cities in India, as well as in rural areas.

The effect is startling, for until that moment the talk had mostly been of parks and gardens and factories, and of benevolent and appreciative rulers. We have to wait until Nirad Chaudhuri's *Passage to England*, published in 1959, for something more explicit.

> I failed to see in England one great distinction which is basic in my country. When I was there I was always asking myself, "Where are the people?" I did so because I was missing the populace, the commonalty, the masses . . .

The attitude might be interpreted as aristocratic; in no country is aristocracy as easy as in India. But we are in reality dealing with something more limiting and less comprehensible: the Indian habit of exclusion, denial, non-seeing. It is part of what Nirad Chaudhuri calls the "ignoble privacy" of Indian social organization; it defines by negatives. It is a lack of wonder, the medieval attribute of a people who are still surrounded by wonders; and in autobiographies this lack of wonder is frequently converted into a hectic self-love.

For its first half Gandhi's autobiography reads like a fairytale. He is dealing with the acknowledged marvels of his early life; and his dry, compressed method, reducing people to their functions and simplified characteristics, reducing places to names and action to a few lines of narrative, turns everything to legend. When the action becomes more complex and political, the method fails; and the book declines more obviously into what it always was: an obsession with vows, food experiments, recurring illness, an obsession with the self. "Thoughts of self," Chaudhuri writes in *The Autobiography of an Unknown Indian*,

> are encouraged by a religious view of life, because it emphasizes our lone coming into the world and our lone exit from it and induces us to judge values in their relation to the individual voyager, the individual voyage, and the ultimate individual destiny.

In *Punjabi Century* Prakash Tandon seems to set out to tell the story of the transformation of the Punjab from 1857 to 1947. He barely attempts the theme. He minutely describes festivals, marriage customs, his father's engineering duties, the various family houses; and the book is transformed into a tribute to his province, his caste, his family and himself: it contains an embarrassing account of his courtship in Sweden, to which is added an injured and recognizably Indian account of his difficulties in getting a job. "Friends not only in my own country but scattered on three continents have suggested I should write my memoirs," Sir Mirza Ismail says.

> It is not easy, however, to write about oneself, and partly for this reason, and partly in order to make the memoirs more interesting, I have quoted from letters received.

Not a few of these letters are tributes to the writer. "You're a wonder!" writes Lord Willingdon. "I would like to name a road after you," writes the Maharaja of Jaipur.

An old-fashioned Muslim vizier, a modern Hindu business-man, the Mahatma: assorted personalities, but recognizably of the same culture. "Writing an autobiography is a practice pecu-liar to the West," a "God-fearing" friend said to Gandhi on the Mahatma's day of silence. "I know of nobody in the East hav-ing written one except amongst those who have come under western influence." And it is in this bastard form—in which a religious view of life, laudable in one culture, is converted steadily into self-love, disagreeable in another culture—that we can begin to see the misunderstandings and futility of the Indo-English encounter.

The civilizations were, and remain, opposed; and the use of English heightens the confusion. When Gandhi came to England for the Round Table Conference in 1931 he stayed for a night at a Quaker guest-house in the Ribble Valley. The garden was in bloom. In the evening Gandhi, in sandals, dhoti and shawl, walked among the flowers. He scarcely looked at them. The story is told by Tandon, who got it from the warden.

> I consoled him that it was quite characteristic of Gandhiji that though he passionately advocated a return to nature he completely lacked interest in its beauty.

But was it strictly a "return to nature" that Gandhi advocated? Wasn't it something more complex? Was Gandhi's aim to re-awaken wonder, or was it rather an unconscious striving after a symbolism acceptable to the Indian masses, a political exploita-tion, however unconscious, of the "ignoble privacy" of Indian attitudes? The Gandhian concept is not easily translated. A "return to nature" and "patriotism": in India the concepts are linked; and the Indian concept of patriotism is unique. Tandon

tells how, in 1919, the Independence movement made its first
impression on his district.

> These visitors spoke about the freedom of India, and this
> intrigued us; but when they talked in familiar analogies and
> idiom about the Kal Yug, we saw what they meant. Had it
> not been prophesied that there were seven eras in India's life
> and history: there had been a Sat Yug, the era of truth, jus-
> tice and prosperity; and then there was to be a Kal Yug, an era
> of falsehood, of demoralization, of slavery and poverty. . . .
> These homely analogies, illustrated by legend and history,
> registered easily, but not so easily the conclusion to which
> they were linked, that it was all the fault of the Angrezi
> Sarkar.

We are in fact dealing with the type of society which Camus
described in the opening chapter of *The Rebel:* a society which
has not learned to see and is incapable of assessing itself, which
asks no questions because ritual and myth have provided all the
answers, a society which has not learned "rebellion." An unfor-
tunate word perhaps, with its juvenile, romantic 1950s associations; but it is the concept which divides, not the East from the
West, but India from almost every other country. It explains
why so much writing about India is unsatisfactory and one-
sided, and it throws into relief the stupendous achievement of
Nirad Chaudhuri's *Autobiography of an Unknown Indian* which,
containing within itself both India and the West, has had the
misfortune of being taken for granted by both sides.

Chaudhuri's *Autobiography* may be the one great book to have
come out of the Indo English encounter. No better account of
the penetration of the Indian mind by the West—and, by extension, of the penetration of one culture by another—will be or
can now be written. It was an encounter which ended in mutual
recoil and futility. For Chaudhuri this futility is an almost per-

sonal tragedy. Yet we can now see that this futility was inevitable. To the static, minutely ordered Indian society, with its pressures ever towards the self, England came less as a political shock than as the source of a New Learning. Chaudhuri quotes from *Rajani*, a Bengali novel by Bankim Chandra Chatterji:

> He did not disclose his business, nor could I ask him out-right. So we discussed social reform and politics. . . . The discussion of ancient literature led in its turn to ancient his-toriography, out of which there emerged some incompara-ble exposition of the classical historians, Tacitus, Plutarch, Thucydides, and others. From the philosophy of history of these writers Amarnath came down to Comte and his *lois des trois états,* which he endorsed. Comte brought in his inter-preter Mill and then Huxley; Huxley brought in Owen and Darwin; and Darwin Buchner and Schopenhauer. Amar-nath poured the most entrancing scholarship into my ears, and I became too engrossed to remember our business.

The astonishing thing about this novel is its date, which is 1877. Kipling's *Plain Tales* were to appear in book form just eleven years later, to reveal the absurdity of this New Learning, nour-ished by books alone. Between the New Learning and its repre-sentatives in Simla there was a gap. Dead civilizations alone ought properly to provide a New Learning. This civilization survived; it had grown suburban and philistine, was soon to become proletarian; and it was fitting that from 1860 to 1910, which Chaudhuri fixes as the period of the Indian Renaissance, the educated Bengali should have been an object of especial ridicule to the English, to whom the unintellectual simplicities of the blue-eyed Pathan were more comprehensible. Chaud-huri, lamenting the death of the Indian Renaissance, and the corrupting, "elemental" Westernization that took its place, pays little attention to this aspect of the encounter.

The élite Indo-English culture of Bengal was as removed

from the Anglo-Indian culture of Simla as it was removed from the culture of the Indian masses. It was a growth of fantasy; the political liberalism it bred could not last. It was to give way to the religious revivalism of a mass movement, to all the combative hocus-pocus of revived "Vedic" traditions such as the launching of ships with coconut-milk instead of champagne, and finally to that cultural confusion which some sentences of Tandon's illustrate so well:

> Gandhi rechristened India Bharat Mata, a name that evoked nostalgic memories, and associated with Gao Mata, the mother cow. ... He ... spoke about the peace of the British as the peace of slavery. Gradually a new picture began to build in our minds, of India coming out of the Kal Yug into a new era of freedom and plenty, Ram Rajya.

Language has at last broken down. Gao Mata, Ram Rajya: for these there are no English equivalents. We can see "national pride" now as an applied phrase, with a special Indian meaning. In the definition of Ram Rajya the true stress falls on "plenty," while "freedom" is an intrusive English *word*. Here is the futility of the Indo-English encounter, the intellectual confusion of the "new" India. This is the great, tragic theme of Chaudhuri's book.

1965

The Last of the Aryans

YOU DON'T have to wait long for the characteristic Nirad Chaudhuri note in *The Continent of Circe*. It occurs, unmistakably, almost before the book begins; yet it has the effect of a climax. There is a frontispiece with two views from the author's verandah in Delhi: one looking up to clouds, one looking down to refugee tents. The title page has a Latin device: *"De rerum indicarum natura: Exempla gentium et seditionum."* The motto—"Know Thyself"—follows, in five Indo-European languages. Seven detailed contents pages come next. And then we come to text: six pages, a chapter almost, headed "In Gratitude." Chaudhuri begins by thanking Khushwant Singh, "the well-known Sikh writer, good companion, and man-about-town, for the loan of his portable typewriter." This seems straightforward enough; but it soon becomes clear that we have to do with an incident.

It is like this. Chaudhuri is tapping away on Khushwant's machine. He is nearing the end of one of the sections of his book and his gratitude to Khushwant, as he says, is at its highest. A "public print" comes his way. It is "the official publication of the American Women's Club of Delhi." It contains "An Interview with Khushwant Singh":

INTERVIEWER: Who is the best Indian writer today?
KHUSHWANT SINGH: In non-fiction? Without a doubt

Nirad Chaudhuri . . . A bitter man, a poor man. He doesn't even own a typewriter. He borrows mine a week at a time.

Chaudhuri is "struck all of a heap":

My poverty is, of course, well known in New Delhi and much further afield, and therefore I was not prepared to see it bruited about by so august a body as the American Women's Club of Delhi.

Khushwant explains. His statement has been given the wrong emphasis. He thought he was only entertaining a lady to tea; he had no idea what her real intention was. He offers Chaudhuri a brand-new portable typewriter as a gift:

I tried to show that I bore no grudge by again borrowing the machine after the publication of the article and by most gratefully accepting the present of the new typewriter.

And a footnote adds:

Having read Pascal early in life I have always tried to profit by his wisdom: *"Si tous les hommes savaient ce quils disaient les uns des autres, il n'y aurait pas quatre amis dans le monde."*

So much about the typewriters on which the book was written; the Americans, though, continue to receive attention for a whole page.

IT IS impossible to take an interest in Nirad Chaudhuri's work without becoming involved with his situation and "personality." This has been his extra-literary creation since the publication in 1951 of his *Autobiography of an Unknown Indian.* The book made him known. But in India it also made him disliked.

Cruelly, it did not lessen his poverty; this mighty work, which in a fairer world would have made its author's fortune and seen him through old age, is now out of print. So, persecuted where not neglected, as he with some reason feels, he sits in Delhi, massively disapproving, more touchy than before, more out of touch with his fellows, never ceasing to attract either the slights of the high or the disagreeable attentions of the low.

His fellow passengers on the Delhi buses wish to know the time. Without inquiry they lift his wrist, consult his wristwatch, and then without acknowledgement let his wrist drop. Sometimes he walks; and, in a land of "massive staticity," where when men walk it is as if "rooted trees were waving in the wind," he walks "in the European manner, that is to say, quickly and with a sense of the goal towards which I am going." Elderly people shout after him, "Left! Right! Left! Right!" Boys call out, "Johnnie Walker!" Sometimes they come right up to him and jeer in Hindi: *"Aré Jahny."* It is not even the Johnnie Walker of the whisky label they refer to, but "a caricature of him by an Indian film star":

> Friends ask me why I do not go for these impertinent young fellows. I reply that I retain my common sense at least to the point of forcing myself to bear all this philosophically. But being also a naturally irascible man, I sometimes breathe a wish that I possessed a flame-thrower and was free to use it. In my conduct and behaviour, however, I never betray this lack of charity.

Indoors it is hardly less dangerous. The London Philharmonic Orchestra comes to Delhi. Chaudhuri talks music to Sir Malcolm Sargent; an English lady whispers to Mrs. Chaudhuri, "What a bold man he is!" He goes to the concert the next day; the British Council has provided tickets. He finds that he is separated from his wife by the aisle. An upper-class Indian lady claims that he is sitting on her chair. She is wrong; she objects then to his proximity; she calls the upper-class usherettes to her aid. He yields; he takes his chair across the aisle to join his wife.

The extra-literary Chaudhuri "personality" is more than a creation of art; the suffering, however self-induced, is too real. Nearly seventy, he is a solitary, in hurtful conflict at every level with his environment.

FAILURE: it is Chaudhuri's obsession. There is the personal failure: twenty years of poverty and humiliation dismissed in a single, moving sentence in the *Autobiography*. There is the failure as a scholar, recorded in the *Autobiography* and echoed in the present book.

> I shall mention the names of four men whom I regard as truly learned. They are Mommsen, Wilamowitz-Moellendorf, Harnack, and Eduard Meyer. When young and immature I cherished the ambition of being the fifth in that series. So I could not have been very modest. But a standard is a standard.

There is the failure, or rather the futility, of the nineteenth-century Anglo-Bengali culture, Chaudhuri's own, set against the larger futility of British rule. These were the interwoven themes of the monumental *Autobiography*. Now Chaudhuri addresses himself to a more encompassing failure: the failure of his country, his race and the land itself, *Aryavarta*, the land of the Aryans.

He has called *The Continent of Circe* an "Essay on the Peoples of India." But his subject is really the Hindus; and his starting-point is the incomprehension, rapidly giving way to rage, which the Hindus have immemorially aroused in non-Hindus. Even E. M. Forster, Chaudhuri says, is more drawn to Muslims; and for all his pro-Indian sentiment, "there are few delineations of the Indian character more insultingly condescending" than those in *A Passage to India*. Forster's plea for Indo-British friendship reminds Chaudhuri of the poem:

> *Turn, turn thy hasty foot aside,*
> *Nor crush that helpless worm!*
> *The frame thy wayward looks deride*
> *Required a God to form.*

"This massive, spontaneous, and uniform criticism by live minds . . . cannot be cancelled by afterthoughts which have their source in the *Untergang des Abendlandes*." And Chaudhuri wishes to cancel nothing. He seeks only to explain. But the act of explaining frequently drives *him* to rage. Where the *Autobiography* was analytic, detached and underplayed, the Essay is strident and tendentious. Chaudhuri's sense of failure and vulnerability, that personality, comes in the way; and it is as a display of personality that *The Continent of Circe* is best to be relished. It is at its most delicious when it is most passionate; and it is most passionate when, one suspects, it is most personal: in the account, for instance, of the "sob-chamber" of Hindu family life, where the only competition is in gloom and people can legitimately consider themselves provoked if they are told they are looking well. So, in Chaudhuri's essay as much as in the work of any uncomprehending foreigner, "Hindu" ends by being almost a word of abuse.

Hindus pacifist? Rubbish, says Chaudhuri. Hindus are militarist, have always been; it is only their inefficiency that makes them less of a menace to the world. To prove this he gives selective historical examples and interprets the frontier conflict with China in a way that will not be faulted in Peking. Again: "The industrial revolution in India at its most disinterested is an expression of anti-European and anti-Western nationalism." This is possible; but it cannot be squared with what immediately follows: "a far stronger force, in actual fact the positive force, is the Hindu's insatiable greed for money." This, at first, seems too

meaningless a statement even for simple denial. But he is making an important point; he is speaking of what some people in
India call the "pigmy mentality" of the Indian capitalist:

> The American industrialist is the old European Conquis-
> tador in a new incarnation. . . . But the Hindu money-maker
> can never be anything but his *paisa*-counting sordid self. . . .
> His spirit is best symbolized by the adulteration of food,
> medicine, and whatever else can be adulterated.

So that the Indian industrial revolution, so far from being an
expression of anti-Western nationalism, turns out to be a very
petty, private thing indeed. Its cynicism might appear to some to
be an extension of caste attitudes. And it might be expected that
Chaudhuri would be critical of caste. Not at all. He asks us to
keep off the caste question if we don't want to pound India to
dust. Caste is the only thing that holds Indian society together.
It is "a natural compensation for man's convergent zoological
evolution and divergent psychological evolution." Caste did not
suppress mobility; that came only with the *Pax Britannica*. And
the Chaudhuri flourish is added:

> If the system suppressed anything it was only ambition
> unrelated to ability, and watching the mischief from this
> kind of ambition in India today I would say that we could do
> with a little more of the caste system in order to put worth-
> less adventurers in their place.

It might seem then that Chaudhuri, in an attempt to make a
whole of Hindu attitudes, has succumbed to any number of
Hindu contradictions. But I also feel that Chaudhuri, living in
Delhi, enduring slights and persecution, has at last succumbed
to what we might call the enemy. He sees India as too big; he has
lost his gift of detachment, his world view. He seeks to expose
where exposure is not really necessary. He has been taken in by

the glitter of "the diplomatic" at Delhi, the flurry of visitors, the cultural displays of competing governments. He exaggerates the importance of India and the interest taken in India. People in England, he says, "are still longing after [India] with the docility of cattle," and the words make sad reading in London in 1965.

BUT THIS is the theme of his polemic: that tropical India is the continent of Circe, drugging and destroying those whom it attracts, and that the Aryans, now Hindus, were the first to be lured from a temperate land, "denatured" and destroyed. Their philosophy is the philosophy of the devitalized. It is rooted in secular distress, the anguish of flesh on the Gangetic plain, where everything quickly decomposes and leads to *tamas*, a comprehensive squalor:

> The tragedy of all the systems of Hindu philosophy is that they confront men with only one choice: remain corruptible and corrupt flesh, or become incorruptible and incorrupt stone.

Be neurotically fussy about cleanliness; or—the greater spirituality—show your indifference to the extent of being able to eat excrement. Hindus are not philosophers; nor do they reverence philosophy. "What we respect are the sadhus, possessors of occult power."

In Chaudhuri's argument it follows without contradiction that a people obsessed with religion, really a "philosophy of sorrow," are obsessed with sex. It is the great anodyne. "Defeat was on the fleshly plane. . . . Rehabilitation must also be in the flesh." The sex act in Hindu sculpture is not symbolic of any sort of spiritual union, as is sometimes said: it is no more than what it appears to be. With a loss of vitality this celebration of the senses declines into the "sex-obsessed chastity of the Hindu, which is perhaps the most despicable ethical notion ever created in the moral evolution of any people":

> Their admiration of the supposed superior sexual knowledge and dexterity of the Hindus is putting ideas in the heads of a particularly depraved set of Occidentals, who are coming to India and working havoc with what sexual sanity . . . we still have.

Well said; but it is on the subject of sex that Chaudhuri becomes most fanciful. Tracing the decline of vitality, he makes too much, one feels, of the emphasis in Sanskrit erotic writings on the pleasures of the *purushayita* or reversed position. Wasn't it in such a position, if one reads right, that Lucius and Fotis first came together in *The Golden Ass?*

Chaudhuri writes of India as though India has never been written about before. He pays little attention to received ideas; he mentions no authorities:

> I am old, and I cannot spend the few years that are left to me tilting at theories which I have taken a lifetime to outgrow. . . . I must therefore be resigned to being called a fool by those who believe in ghosts. . . . Historical conferences in India always remind me of séances.

He places the Aryan settlement of the Gangetic plain in the seventh century B.C. This will be offensive to those Indians who think of India as the Aryan heartland and, playing with millennia, like to think of Rome as a recent, and peripheral, disturbance. He allows no civilization worth the name to the indigenous Australoids, whom he calls the Darks. Rigid barriers were set up against them, and Chaudhuri—going back on some of his old views—claims that no significant intermingling of the races took place. The Darks, in their free or servile state, remain to this day genetically stable; and to this day, it might be added, the burning of a giant effigy of a Dark is the climax of an annual Hindu pageant-play. Hindu *apartheid* quickly gave the Darks the psychology of a subject race. Chaudhuri retells a story from the *Ramayana,* the Hindu epic. It is reported one day to Rama, the Aryan hero, that the son of a brahmin has died suddenly. There can be only one explanation: an act of impiety. Rama goes out to have a look and, sure enough, finds that a young Dark has been performing Aryan religious rites. The Dark is at once decapitated and the brahmin's son comes back to life. In later versions of the story the Dark dies happily: death at the hands of an Aryan is a sure way to heaven. Not even slavery created so complete a subjection.

So that, as Chaudhuri tells it, the continent of Circe has played a cruel joke on the Hindus. The first white people to come into contact with a black race, and the first and most persistent practitioners of *apartheid,* they have themselves, over the centuries, under a punishing sun, grown dark. The snow-capped Himalayas have become objects of pilgrimage; and some Hindus, in their hysteria, look beyond that to the North Pole, of which modern map-makers have made them aware. There, someone will tell you in all the blaze of Madras, there at the North Pole lies the true home of the Hindus:

> The theme of paradise lost and regained is one of the major stories of Hindu mythology, and it must date from the Iranian sojourn of the Indian Aryans. In the stories the gods recover their heaven. . . . But in history paradise is lost for ever; and the curse begins to work: in sorrow shalt thou eat of it all the days of thy life.

This is the true Chaudhuri mood; and, for all Chaudhuri's fanciful flights and parenthetic rages, it must be respected: the Hindu sense of exile and loss is real. Yet the layman must ask certain questions. Chaudhuri places the Aryan settlement just two or three generations before the birth of the Buddha. Could the philosophy of sorrow and the devitalization of the Aryan have occurred so soon? Could the Aryan, even the settler in the South, have undertaken the colonization of South-east Asia a thousand years later? The reader of Chaudhuri's book, working from Chaudhuri's clues, might easily come to a different conclusion from Chaudhuri. He might feel that the Hindus, so far from being denatured Aryans, have continued, in their curious and self-willed isolation, to be close to their elemental Aryan origins. For the Aryan in India, Chaudhuri says, both sensibility and effort became parts of piety; and this surely makes many Hindu attitudes less mysterious. The attitudes remain; the gloss varies with historical circumstance. Chaudhuri writes with some sharpness of Hindus who now use European rationalism to excuse their "irrational urges and taboos." Yet we have seen how he himself uses a borrowed language to defend caste, a primitive institution. Hindus can be found today to defend Gandhi's assassination on the grounds that the assassin was a brahmin. This is outrageous; but it becomes intelligible and logical if we see it as an extension of the old Aryan approval of Rama's slaying of the impious, and complaisant, Dark in the *Ramayana* story.

And there is the erotic sculpture. It cannot be ignored. It cannot be talked away. It is too widespread, too casual. It is of a piece with the open sensuality of the *Rig Veda*, the earliest Hindu sacred book. This has been called the first recorded speech of Aryan man. Chaudhuri translates a sample:

> *He achieves not—he whose penis hangs limp between his thighs;*
> *Achieves he alone whose hairy thing swells up when he lies.*

It is Indrani, the Queen Goddess, who speaks; and she is a match for her consort who, for his lechery, was punished by the appearance all over his body of a thousand *pudenda muliebria*. This is a campfire, peasant lewdness. And when all is said and done this is what *aryan* means: he is one who tills the soil.

Chaudhuri's plea that Hindus should turn their backs on Asia and recover their Aryan or European personality is, if narrowly interpreted, meaningless. Part of the trouble is that Chaudhuri makes "Aryan" and "European" interchangeable. But "European" surely needs to be more closely defined, and dated. It is a developing concept; "Aryan" is fixed. And Chaudhuri's plea becomes very thin indeed when we find that for *Homo europaeus* in his present predominant and proliferating variety Chaudhuri has no high regard:

> The most vapid and insignificant class of human beings which so far has been evolved in history [is] the modern urban lower middle class of the West.

The absurd thing is that in India Aryan racial pride still has point; in Europe it has little. Of this pride Chaudhuri's book might be seen as the latest expression. He is not European; with his poetic feeling for rivers and cattle, his insistence on caste, he remains Aryan.

> Make a European society with India's religion. Become an occidental of occidentals in your spirit of equality, freedom, work, and energy, and at the same time a Hindu to the very backbone in religious culture, and instincts.

This is not Chaudhuri. It is Vivekananda, the Vedantist, writing at the turn of the century. A Bengali, like Chaudhuri, a reformer, a product of the Anglo-Bengali culture; and the message, with all its imprecisions and contradictions, is like Chaudhuri's. The Anglo-Bengali culture survives. To its passionate introspection *The Continent of Circe* is a late addition, quirky, at times wild, but rich and always stimulating.

1966

Theatrical Natives

THE KIPLING revival is curious. It seems to be mainly academic—and therefore self-perpetuating—and its interest seems to be less in the work than in the man. Kipling is more complex than his legend. It is easy for the critic to be made possessive by this discovery and to go through the work just looking for clues. It can be shown, for instance, from a story like "The Bridge-Builders," that Kipling was not insensitive to the subtleties of Hindu iconography. The fact is interesting, but it doesn't make the story any less obscure or unsatisfactory. The fact is also awkward: it doesn't fit with other facts. And so it happens that attempts to set the legend right often end in simple tabulation, of matter and motif. This is the method of Mr. Stewart's *Rudyard Kipling*, which does little more than celebrate a reading of the Kipling canon.

The legend survives. "The Kipling That Nobody Read"— the title of Mr. Edmund Wilson's essay—is still the Kipling nobody reads. Kipling revaluations are self-defeating, since they lead back more surely to the only Kipling of value, which is the Kipling of the legend. It is the legend of the brief serene decade of British India, when the Mutiny finally became a memory and nationalism was still to come: a moment of order and romance, vanishing even as it was apprehended, later to embarrass, sadden, anger and be explained away, until it became historical. The legend can be accepted now. Mr. Cornell accepts it: it is one of the merits of his book. *Kipling in India* is the most balanced analysis I have read of Kipling's literary achievement. Mr. Cornell says that his subject is Kipling's apprenticeship, which contained the legendary achievement: the fixing, for all time, of that moment of British India.

It was the unlikely achievement of a very young man who took his unimportant journalistic work seriously; who abandoned the graver literary ambitions of his school-days to become a kind of club-writer; who aimed at ordinariness, and feared above all to offend. The club was at first the Punjab Club, of which Kipling became a member at seventeen. Soon it was all British India. This artificial, complete and homogeneous world did not require explanations. "Dedication," Mr. Cornell says, "walked hand in hand with triviality." The triviality was the triviality of "good-fellowship, not savage mockery"; there were limits to self-satire. Kipling followed the rules and didn't sink. Like the Lama in *Kim,* he acquired merit.

Mr. Cornell is right to stress the club, for it is from his function as a club-writer that Kipling's virtues came, and especially that allusive, elliptical prose, easy but packed, which, almost one hundred years later, still seems so new. Mr. Cornell's account of the development of this prose is fascinating. This is Kipling at seventeen, describing a Hindu pageant in Lahore:

To the great delight of the people, Ramachandra and his brothers, attired in the traditional costume and head-dress, were mounted aloft and held the mighty bow, the breaking of which shook the world to its centre. But it must be admitted that Sita, uncomfortably astride a broad-backed wickerwork bull, supported by an uneasy Rama, buried in tinsel and attended by bearers . . . was a spectacle more comic than imposing.

This, as Mr. Cornell says, is cheap, obvious and anonymous. It is without Kipling's later "visual clarity." It is also the work of an outsider: the Anglo-Indian was closer to the country. But two years later the tone changes. Here is another fair scene:

> Presently the bolder spirits among them would put out a horny finger, and carefully touch one of the bullocks. Then as the animal was evidently constructed of nothing more terrible than clay . . . the whole hand would be drawn gently over its form; and, after an appreciative pat, the adventurous one would begin a lengthy dissertation to the bystanders at large.

The outsider has drawn closer. And sixteen months later the prose is like this:

> Suddhoo sleeps on the roof generally, except when he sleeps in the street. He used to go to Peshawar in the cold weather to visit his son who sells curiosities near the Edwardes' Gate, and then he slept under a real mud roof. Suddhoo is a great friend of mine, because his cousin had a son who secured, thanks to my recommendation, the post of head-messenger to a big firm in the Station. Suddhoo says that God will make me a Lieutenant-Governor one of these days. I daresay his prophecy will come true.

This is the accomplished club-writer. He has mastered his subject and he knows his audience. He deals in an irony so private it might be missed by an outsider. To the Anglo-Indian, as Mr. Cornell points out, simple phrases like "a great friend of mine" and "a real mud roof" would have precise meanings. On the difference between the first and last quotations, he writes:

> In the earlier piece, Indian life appeared as no more than a passing show to be judged and dismissed on its aesthetic

merits by a superior—and very young—English spectator. In the 1886 story, however, Kipling has penetrated to the heart of the Anglo-Indian's historical dilemma with amazing swiftness and economy.

The judgment is typical of Mr. Cornell's balance and perception. He has not been tempted to make use of "The House of Suddhoo" to amend the legend; he makes a *literary* judgment, and it is correct.

Kipling's prose was later to go beyond this. It was to become a superb instrument of narration, concise, full of flavour and speed, and wonderfully pictorial. But the club-writer always needed the club, the common points of reference; he needed the legend, which perhaps his own stories had helped to create. Kipling can best be savoured in a group of related stories: to this extent the tabulators are justified. A story by Chekhov is complete in itself; a story by Kipling isn't. It is either too slight or too long-windedly anecdotal. A legitimate delay in an Indian story would lose its point elsewhere.

There were the usual blue-and-white striped jail-made rugs on the uneven floor; the usual glass-studded Amritsar *phulkaris* draped to nails driven into the flaking whitewash of the walls; the usual half-dozen chairs that did not match, picked up at sales of dead men's effects. . . . The little windows, fifteen feet up, were darkened with wasp-nests, and lizards hunted flies between the beams of the wood-ceiled roof.

"William the Conqueror," from which the passage is taken (it is quoted by Mr. Stewart), is not a good story. It is pure comic-strip and—it is a love story set against a background of famine and corpses—it is horrifying to some. But details like these make it a true and acceptable part of Kipling's Indian work. In another setting comparable details would tell less. They wouldn't be as intimate; the "usual" would have less meaning; and "dead men's effects" would not speak of that dedication which was part of the Anglo-Indian's myth. Kipling's Anglo-Indians are always slightly embarrassing when they are on leave in England; there is a similar embarrassment, of ordinariness, it might be said, even in an Indian story like "The Gadsbys," from which India is almost totally subtracted.

Just as in that passage detail adds to detail, and we would be without none of them, so each of Kipling's Indian stories adds to the others and is supported by them. Kipling's stories are not like Chekhov's; they are like Turgenev's hunting sketches or Angus Wilson's stories of the late forties. They make one big book; they have to be taken together. They catch—or create—a complete society at a particular moment. It is in its search for the independent, good Kipling story that Kipling criticism becomes aggressive and tabulatory. Even Mr. Cornell succumbs. He notices the frequency of disguises, hoaxes and frauds in the stories; and he makes much of this. He should have ignored it. The fact would have been important if Kipling were more interested in people than in the types with whom he filled his club, never allowing himself satire, mockery or anger beyond what the club permitted. As it is, such tabulation shows up the limitations of the too homogeneous club as a source for material, and it shows up the limitations of the club-writer, whose closest literary friend, later in England, was to be Rider Haggard.

The irony, like the legend, remains. The "long-coated theatrical natives discussing metaphysics in English and Bengali"— threats to order and romance, and therefore to be ceaselessly satirized—were to lead to a writer like Nirad Chaudhuri and a film maker like Ray. The club has disappeared. By becoming its spokesman and jester, by brilliantly creating its legend, Kipling made the disappearance of the club certain.

1966

Conrad's Darkness and Mine

IT HAS TAKEN me a long time to come round to Conrad. And if I begin with an account of his difficulty, it is because I have to be true to my experience of him. I would find it hard to be detached about Conrad. He was, I suppose, the first modern writer I was introduced to. It was through my father. My father was a self-taught man, picking his way through a cultural confusion of which he was perhaps hardly aware and which I have only recently begun to understand; and he wished himself to be a writer. He read less for pleasure than for clues, hints and encouragement; and he introduced me to those writers he had come upon in his own search. Conrad was one of the earliest of these: Conrad the stylist, but more than that, Conrad the late starter, holding out hope to those who didn't seem to be starting at all.

I believe I was ten when Conrad was first read to me. It sounds alarming; but the story was "The Lagoon"; and the reading was a success. "The Lagoon" is perhaps the only story of Conrad's that can be read to a child. It is very short, about fifteen pages. A forest-lined tropical river at dusk. The white man in the boat says, "We'll spend the night in Arsat's clearing." The boat swings into a creek; the creek opens out into a lagoon. A lonely house on the shore; inside, a woman is dying. And during the night Arsat, the young man who is her lover, will tell how they both came there. It is a story of illicit love in another place, an abduction, a chase, the death of a brother, abandoned to the pursuers. What Arsat has to say should take no more than fifteen minutes; but romance is romance, and when Arsat's story ends the dawn comes up; the early-morning breeze blows away the mist; the woman is dead. Arsat's happiness, if it existed, has been flawed and brief; and now he will leave the lagoon and go back to his own place, to meet his fate. The white man, too, has to go. And the last picture is of Arsat, alone in his lagoon, looking "beyond the great light of a cloudless day into the darkness of a world of illusions."

In time the story of "The Lagoon" became blurred. But the sense of night and solitude and doom stayed with me, grafted, in my fantasy, to the South Sea or tropical island setting of the Sabu and Jon Hall films. I have, unwillingly, looked at "The Lagoon" again. There is a lot of Conrad in it—passion and the abyss, solitude and futility and the world of illusions—and I am not sure now that it isn't the purest piece of fiction Conrad wrote. The brisk narrative, the precise pictorial writing, the setting of river and hidden lagoon, the nameless white visitor, the story during the night of love and loss, the death at daybreak: everything comes beautifully together. And if I say it is a pure piece of fiction, it is because the story speaks for itself; the writer does not come between his story and the reader.

"The Lagoon" was parodied by Max Beerbohm in "A Christmas Garland." Writers' myths can depend on accidents like that. "The Lagoon," as it happens, was the first short story Conrad wrote; and though later, when I read the parody, I was able to feel that I was in the know about Conrad, from my own point of view "The Lagoon" had been a cheat. Because I was never to find anything so strong and direct in Conrad again.

There is a story, "Karain," written not long after "The Lagoon." It has the same Malayan setting and, as Conrad acknowledged, a similar motif. Karain, inspired by sudden sexual jealousy, kills the friend whose love quest he had promised to serve; and thereafter Karain is haunted by the ghost of the man he has killed. One day he meets a wise old man, to whom he confesses. The old man exorcises the ghost; and Karain, with the old man as his counsellor, becomes a warrior and a conqueror, a ruler. The old man dies; the ghost of the murdered friend returns to haunt Karain. He is immediately lost; his power and splendor are nothing; he swims out to the white men's ship and asks them, unbelievers from another world, for help. They give him a charm: a Jubilee sixpence. The charm works; Karain becomes a man again.

The story is, on the surface, a yarn about native superstition. But to Conrad it is much more; it is profounder, and more wonderful, than "The Lagoon"; and he is determined that its whole meaning should be grasped. All the suggestions that were implicit in "The Lagoon" are now spelled out. The white men have names; they talk, and act as a kind of chorus. So we are asked to contemplate the juxtaposition of two cultures, one open and without belief, one closed and ruled by old magic; one, "on the edge of outer darkness," exploring the world, one imprisoned in a small part of it. But illusions are illusions, mirage is mirage. Isn't London itself, the life of its streets, a mirage? "I see it. It is there; it pants, it runs; it rolls; it is strong and alive; it would smash you if you didn't look out; but I'll be hanged if it is yet as real to me as the other thing." So, romantically and somewhat puzzlingly, the story ends.

The simple yarn is made to carry a lot. It requires a more complex response than the plainer fiction of "The Lagoon." Sensations—night and solitude and doom—are not enough; the writer wishes to involve us in more than his fantasy; we are required—the chorus or commentary requires us—to stand outside the facts of the story and contemplate the matter. The story has become a kind of parable. Nothing has been rigged, though, because nothing is being proved; only wonder is being awakened.

In a preface to a later collection of stories Conrad wrote: "The romantic feeling of reality was in me an inborn faculty." He hadn't deliberately sought out romantic subjects; they had offered themselves to him:

I have a natural right to [my subjects] because my past is very much my own. If their course lies out of the beaten path of organized social life, it is, perhaps, because I myself did in a sort break away from it early in obedience to an impulse which must have been very genuine since it has sustained me through all the dangers of disillusion. But that origin of my literary work was very far from giving a larger scope to my imagination. On the contrary, the mere fact of dealing with matters outside the general run of every day experience laid me under the obligation of a more scrupulous fidelity to the truth of my own sensations. The problem was to make unfamiliar things credible. To do that I had to create for them, to reproduce for them, to envelop them in their proper atmosphere of actuality. This was the hardest task of all and the most important, in view of that conscientious rendering of truth in thought and fact which has been always my aim.

But the truths of that story, "Karain," are difficult ones. The world of illusions, men as prisoners of their cultures, belief and unbelief: these are truths one has to be ready for, and perhaps half possess already, because the story does not carry them convincingly within itself. The suggestion that the life of London is as much a mirage as the timeless life of the Malayan archipelago is puzzling, because the two-page description of the London streets with which the story ends is too literal: blank faces, hansom cabs, omnibuses, girls "talking vivaciously," "dirty men . . . discussing filthily," a policeman. There isn't anything in that catalogue that can persuade us that the life described is a mirage.

Reality hasn't fused with the writer's fantasy. The concept of the mirage has to be applied; it is a matter of words, a disturbing caption to a fairly straight picture.

I have considered this simple story at some length because it illustrates, in little, the difficulties I was to have with the major works. I felt with Conrad I wasn't getting the point. Stories, simple in themselves, always seemed at some stage to elude me. And there were the words, the words that issued out of the writer's need to be faithful to the truth of his own sensations. The words got in the way; they obscured. *The Nigger of the Narcissus* and *Typhoon*, famous books, were impenetrable.

In 1896 the young H. G. Wells, in an otherwise kind review of *An Outcast of the Islands*, the book before *The Nigger*, wrote: "Mr Conrad is wordy; his story is not so much told as seen intermittently through a haze of sentences. He has still to learn the great half of his art, the art of leaving things unwritten." Conrad wrote a friendly letter to Wells; but on the same day—the story is in Jocelyn Baines's biography—he wrote to Edward Garnett: "Something brings the impression off—makes its effect. What? It can be nothing but the expression—the arrangement of words, the style." It is, for a novelist, an astonishing definition of style. Because style in the novel, and perhaps in all prose, is more than an "arrangement of words": it is an arrangement, even an orchestration, of perceptions, it is a matter of knowing where to put what. But Conrad aimed at fidelity. Fidelity required him to be explicit.

It is this explicitness, this unwillingness to let the story speak for itself, this anxiety to draw all the mystery out of a straightforward situation, that leads to the mystification of *Lord Jim*. It isn't always easy to know what is being explained. The story is usually held to be about honour. I feel myself that it is about the theme—much more delicate in 1900 than today—of the racial straggler. And, such is Conrad's explicitness, both points of view can be supported by quotation. *Lord Jim*, however, is an imperialist book, and it may be that the two points of view are really one.

Whatever the mystery of *Lord Jim,* it wasn't of the sort that could hold me. Fantasy, imagination, story if you like, had been refined away by explicitness. There was something unbalanced, even unfinished, about Conrad. He didn't seem able to go beyond his first simple conception of a story; his invention seemed to fail so quickly. And even in his variety there was something tentative and uncertain.

There was *The Secret Agent,* a police thriller that seemed to end almost as soon as it began, with a touch of Arnold Bennett and *Riceyman Steps* in that Soho interior, and a Wellsian jokeyness about London street names and cabbies and broken-down horses—as though, when dealing with the known, the written about, the gift of wonder left the writer and he had to depend on other writers' visions. There was *Under Western Eyes,* which, with its cast of Russian revolutionaries and its theme of betrayal, promised to be Dostoevskyan but then dissolved away into analysis. There was the too set-up fiction of *Victory:* the pure, aloof man rescues a girl from a musical company touring the East and takes her to a remote island, where disaster, in the form of gangsters, will come to them. And there was *Nostromo,* about South America, a confusion of characters and themes, which I couldn't get through at all.

A multiplicity of Conrads, and they all seemed to me to be flawed. The hero of *Victory,* holding himself aloof from the world, had "refined away everything except disgust"; and it seemed to me that in his fictions Conrad had refined away, as commonplace, those qualities of imagination and fantasy and invention that I went to novels for. The Conrad novel was like a simple film with an elaborate commentary. A film: the characters and settings could be seen very clearly. But realism often required trivial incidental dialogue, the following of trivial actions; the melodramatic flurry at the end emphasized the slowness and bad proportions of what had gone before; and the commentary emphasized the fact that the characters were actors.

BUT WE read at different times for different things. We take to novels our own ideas of what the novel should be; and those ideas are made by our needs, our education, our background or perhaps our ideas of our background. Because we read, really, to find out what we already know, we can take a writer's virtues for granted. And his originality, the news he is offering us, can go over our heads.

It came to me that the great novelists wrote about highly organized societies. I had no such society; I couldn't share the assumptions of the writers; I didn't see my world reflected in theirs. My colonial world was more mixed and secondhand, and more restricted. The time came when I began to ponder the mystery—Conradian word—of my own background: that island in the mouth of a great South American river, the Orinoco, one of the Conradian dark places of the earth, where my father had conceived literary ambitions for himself and then for me, but from which, in my mind, I had stripped all romance and perhaps even reality: preferring to set "The Lagoon," when it was read to me, not on the island I knew, with its muddy rivers, mangrove and swamps, but somewhere far away.

It seemed to me that those of us who were born there were curiously naked, that we lived purely physically. It wasn't an easy thing to explain, even to oneself. But in Conrad, in that very story of "Karain," I was later to find my feelings about the land exactly caught.

And really, looking at that place, landlocked from the sea and shut off from the land by the precipitous slopes of mountains, it was difficult to believe in the existence of any neighbourhood. It was still, complete, unknown, and full of a life that went on stealthily with a troubling effect of solitude; of a life that seemed unaccountably empty of anything that would stir the thought, touch the heart, give a hint of the ominous sequence of days. It appeared to us a land without memories, regrets, and hopes; a land where nothing could survive the coming of the night, and where each sunrise, like a dazzling act of special creation, was disconnected from the eve and the morrow.

It is a passage that, earlier, I would have hurried through: the purple passage, the reflective caption. Now I see a precision in its romanticism, and a great effort of thought and sympathy. And the effort doesn't stop with the aspect of the land. It extends to all men in these dark or remote places who, for whatever reason, are denied a clear vision of the world: Karain himself, in his world of phantoms; Wang, the self-exiled Chinese of *Victory*, self-contained within the "instinctive existence" of the Chinese peasant; the two Belgian empire builders of "An Outpost of Progress," helpless away from their fellows, living in the middle of Africa "like blind men in a large room, aware only of what came in contact with them, but unable to see the general aspect of things."

"An Outpost of Progress" is now to me the finest thing Conrad wrote. It is the story of two commonplace Belgians, new to the new Belgian Congo, who find that they have unwittingly, through their negro assistant, traded Africans for ivory, are then abandoned by the surrounding tribesmen, and go mad. But my first judgement of it had been only literary. It had seemed familiar; I had read other stories of lonely white men going mad in hot countries. And my rediscovery, or discovery, of Conrad really began with one small scene in *Heart of Darkness*.

The African background—"the demoralized land" of plunder and licensed cruelty—I took for granted. That is how we can be imprisoned by our assumptions. The background now seems to me to be the most effective part of the book; but then it was no more than what I expected. The story of Kurtz, the upriver ivory agent, who is led to primitivism and lunacy by his unlimited power over primitive men, was lost on me. But there was a page which spoke directly to me, and not only of Africa.

The steamer is going upriver to meet Kurtz; it is "like travelling back to the earliest beginnings of the world." A hut is sighted on the bank. It is empty, but it contains one book, sixty years old. *An Inquiry into Some Points of Seamanship,* tattered, without covers, but "lovingly stitched afresh with white cotton thread." And in the midst of nightmare, this old book, "dreary ... with illustrative diagrams and repulsive tables of figures," but with its "singleness of intention," its "honest concern for the right way of going to work," seems to the narrator to be "luminous with another than a professional light."

This scene, perhaps because I have carried it for so long, or perhaps because I am more receptive to the rest of the story, now makes less of an impression. But I suppose that at the time it answered something of the political panic I was beginning to feel.

To be a colonial was to know a kind of security; it was to inhabit a fixed world. And I suppose that in my fantasy I had seen myself coming to England as to some purely literary region, where, untrammelled by the accidents of history or background, I could make a romantic career for myself as a writer. But in the new world I felt that ground move below me. The new politics, the curious reliance of men on institutions they were yet working to undermine, the simplicity of beliefs and the hideous simplicity of actions, the corruption of causes, half-made societies that seemed doomed to remain half-made: these were the things that began to preoccupy me. They were not things from which I could detach myself. And I found that Conrad—sixty years before, in the time of a great peace—had been everywhere before me. Not as a man with a cause, but a man offering, as in *Nostromo,* a vision of the world's half-made societies as places which continuously made and unmade themselves, where there was no goal, and where always "something inherent in the necessities of successful action . . . carried with it the moral degradation of the idea." Dismal, but deeply felt: a kind of truth and half a consolation.

To understand Conrad, then, it was necessary to begin to match his experience. It was also necessary to lose one's preconceptions of what the novel should do and, above all, to rid oneself of the subtle corruptions of the novel or comedy of manners. When art copies life, and life in its turn mimics art, a writer's originality can often be obscured. *The Secret Agent* seemed to be a thriller. But Inspector Heat, correct but oddly disturbing, was like no policeman before in fiction—though there have been many like him since. And, in spite of appearances, this grand lady, patroness of a celebrated anarchist, was not Lady Bracknell:

> His views had nothing in them to shock or startle her, since she judged them from the standpoint of her lofty position. Indeed, her sympathies were easily accessible to a man of that sort. She was not an exploiting capitalist herself; she was, as it were, above the play of economic conditions. And she had a great pity for the more obvious forms of common human miseries, precisely because she was such a complete stranger to them that she had to translate her conception into terms of mental suffering before she could grasp the notion of their cruelty. . . . She had come to believe almost his theory of the future, since it was not repugnant to her prejudices. She disliked the new element of plutocracy in the social compound, and industrialism as a method of human development appeared to her singularly repulsive in its mechanical and unfeeling character. The humanitarian hopes of the mild Michaelis tended not towards utter destruction, but merely towards the economic ruin of the system. And she did not really see where was the moral harm of it. It would do away with all the multitude of the parvenus, whom she disliked and mistrusted, not because they had arrived anywhere (she denied that), but because of their profound

unintelligence of the world, which was the primary cause of
the crudity of their perceptions and the aridity of their hearts.

Not Lady Bracknell. Someone much more real, and still recognizable in more than one country. Younger today perhaps;
but humanitarian concern still disguises a similar arrogance and
simplicity, the conviction that wealth, a particular fortune, position or a particular name are the only possible causes of human
self-esteem. And in how many countries today can we find the
likeness of this man?

> The all but moribund veteran of dynamite wars had been
> a great actor in his time. . . . The famous terrorist had never
> in his life raised personally so much as his little finger against
> the social edifice. He was no man of action. . . . With a more
> subtle intention, he took the part of an insolent and ven-
> omous evoker of sinister impulses which lurk in the blind
> envy and exasperated vanity of ignorance, in the suffering
> and misery of poverty, in all the hopeful and noble illusions
> of righteous anger, pity and revolt. The shadow of his evil
> gift clung to him yet like the smell of a deadly drug in an old
> vial of poison, emptied now, useless, ready to be thrown
> away upon the rubbish-heap of things that had served their
> time.

The phrase that had struck me there was "sinister impulses
which lurk in . . . noble illusions." But now another phrase
stands out: the "exasperated vanity of ignorance." It is so with
the best of Conrad. Words which at one time we disregard, at
another moment glitter.

But the character in *The Secret Agent* who is the subject of
that paragraph hardly exists outside that paragraph. His name is
Karl Yundt; he is not one of the figures we remember. Physically, he is a grotesque, a caricature, as are so many of the
others, for all Conrad's penetration—anarchists, policemen,

government ministers. There is nothing in Karl Yundt's dramatic appearance in the novel, so to speak, that matches the profundity of that paragraph or hints at the quality of reflection out of which he was created.

My reservations about Conrad as a novelist remain. There is something flawed and unexercised about his creative imagination. He does not—except in *Nostromo* and some of the stories—involve me in his fantasy; and *Lord Jim* is still to me more acceptable as a narrative poem than as a novel. Conrad's value to me is that he is someone who sixty to seventy years ago meditated on my world, a world I recognize today. I feel this about no other writer of the century. His achievement derives from the honesty which is part of his difficulty, that "scrupulous fidelity to the truth of my own sensations."

Nothing is rigged in Conrad. He doesn't remake countries. He chose, as we now know, incidents from real life; and he meditated on them. "Meditate" is his own, exact word. And what he says about his heroine in *Nostromo* can be applied to himself. "The wisdom of the heart having no concern with the erection or demolition of theories any more than with the defence of prejudices, has no random words at its command. The words it pronounces have the value of acts of integrity, tolerance and compassion."

EVERY GREAT writer is produced by a series of special circumstances. With Conrad these circumstances are well known: his Polish youth, his twenty years of wandering, his settling down to write in his late thirties, experience more or less closed, in England, a foreign country. These circumstances have to be considered together; one cannot be stressed above any other. The fact of the late start cannot be separated from the background and the scattered experience. But the late start is important.

Most imaginative writers discover themselves, and their world, through their work. Conrad, when he settled down to write, was, as he wrote to the publisher William Blackwood, a man whose character had been formed. He knew his world, and had reflected on his experience. Solitariness, passion, the abyss: the themes are constant in Conrad. There is a unity in a writer's work; but the Conrad who wrote *Victory*, though easier and more direct in style, was no more experienced and wise than the Conrad who, twenty years before, had written *Almayer's Folly*. His uncertainties in the early days seem to have been mainly literary, a trying out of subjects and moods. In 1896, the year after the publication of *Almayer's Folly*, he could break off from the romantic turgidities of *The Rescue* and not only write "The Lagoon," but also begin "An Outpost of Progress." These stories, which stand at the opposite ends, as it were, of my comprehension of Conrad, one story so romantic, one so brisk and tough, were written almost at the same time.

And there are the aphorisms. They run right through Conrad's work, and their tone never varies. It is the same wise man who seems to be speaking. "The fear of finality which lurks in every human breast and prevents so many heroisms and so many crimes": that is from *Almayer's Folly*, 1895. And this is from *Nostromo*, 1904: "a man to whom love comes late, not as the most splendid of illusions, but like an enlightening and priceless misfortune"—which is almost too startling in the context. From *The Secret Agent*, 1907, where it seems almost wasted: "Curiosity being one of the forms of self-revelation, a systematically incurious person remains always partly mysterious." And lastly, from *Victory*, 1915: "the fatal imperfection of all the gifts of life, which makes of them a delusion and a snare"—which might have been fitted into any of the earlier books.

To take an interest in a writer's work is, for me, to take an interest in his life; one interest follows automatically on the other. And to me there is something peculiarly depressing about Conrad's writing life. With a writer like Ibsen one can be as unsettled by the life as by the plays themselves. One wonders about the surrender of the life of the senses; one wonders about the short-lived satisfactions of the creative instinct, as unappeasable as the senses. But with Ibsen there is always the excitement of the work, developing, changing, enriched by these very doubts and conflicts. All Conrad's subjects, and all his conclusions, seem to have existed in his head when he settled down to write. *Nostromo* could be suggested by a few lines in a book, *The Secret Agent* by a scrap of conversation and a book. But, really, experience was in the past; and the labour of the writing life lay in dredging up this experience, in "casting round"—Conradian words—for suitable subjects for meditation.

Conrad's ideas about fiction seem to have shaped early during his writing career. And, whatever the uncertainties of his early practice, these ideas never changed. In 1895, when his first book was published, he wrote to a friend, who was also beginning to write: "All the charm, all the truth of [your story] are thrown away by the construction—by the mechanism (so to speak) of the story which makes it appear false. . . . You have much imagination: much more than I ever will have if I live to be a hundred years old. Well, that imagination (I wish I had it) should be used to create human souls: to disclose human hearts—and not to create events that are properly speaking *accidents* only. To accomplish it you must cultivate your poetic faculty . . . you must squeeze out of yourself every sensation, every thought, every image." When he met Wells, Conrad said (the story is Wells's): "My dear Wells, what is this *Love and Mr Lewisham* about? What is all this about Jane Austen? What is it all *about*?" And later—all these quotations are from Jocelyn Baines's biography—Conrad was to write: "The national English novelist seldom regards his work—the exercise of his Art—as an achievement of active life by which he will produce certain definite effects upon the emotions of his readers, but simply as an instinctive, often unreasoned, outpouring of his own emotions."

Were these ideas of Conrad's French and European? Conrad, after all, liked Balzac, most breathless of writers; and

Balzac, through instinct and unreason, a man bewitched by his own society, had arrived at something very like that "romantic feeling of reality" which Conrad said was his own inborn faculty. It seems at least possible that, in his irritated rejection of the English novel of manners and the novel of "accidents," Conrad was rationalizing what was at once his own imaginative deficiency as well as his philosophical need to stick as close as possible to the facts of every situation. In fiction he did not seek to discover; he sought only to explain; the discovery of every tale, as the narrator of *Under Western Eyes* says, is a moral one.

In the experience of most writers the imaginative realizing of a story constantly modifies the writer's original concept of it. Out of experience, fantasy and all kinds of impulses, a story suggests itself. But the story has to be tested by, and its various parts survive, the writer's dramatic imagination. Things work or they don't work; what is true feels true; what is false is false. And the writer, trying to make his fiction work, making accommodations with his imagination, can say more than he knows. With Conrad the story seems to be fixed; it is something given, like the prose "argument" stated at the beginning of a section of an old poem. Conrad knows exactly what he has to say. And sometimes, as in *Lord Jim* and *Heart of Darkness,* he says less than he intends.

Heart of Darkness breaks into two. There is the reportage about the Congo, totally accurate, as we now know: Conrad scholarship has been able to identify almost everyone in that story. And there is the fiction, which in the context is like fiction, about Kurtz, the ivory agent who allows himself to become a kind of savage African god. The idea of Kurtz, when it is stated, seems good: he will show "what particular region of the first ages a man's untrammelled feet may take him into by way of solitude." Beguiling words, but they are abstract; and the idea, deliberately worked out, remains an applied idea. Conrad's attitude to fiction—not as something of itself, but as a varnish on fact—is revealed by his comment on the story. "It is experience pushed a little (and only very little) beyond the actual facts of the case for the perfectly legitimate, I believe, purpose of bringing it home to the minds and bosoms of the reader."

Mystery—it is the Conradian word. But there is no mystery in the work itself, the things imagined; mystery remains a concept of the writer's. The theme of passion and the abyss recurs in Conrad, but there is nothing in his work like the evening scene in Ibsen's *Ghosts:* the lamp being lit, the champagne being called for, light and champagne only underlining the blight of that house, a blight that at first seems external and arbitrary and is then seen to come from within. There is no scene like that, which takes us beyond what we witness and becomes a symbol for aspects of our own experience. There is nothing—still on the theme of blight—like "The Withered Arm," Hardy's story of rejection and revenge and the dereliction of the innocent, which goes beyond the country tale of magic on which it was based. Conrad is too particular and concrete a writer for that; he sticks too close to the facts; if he had meditated on those stories he might have turned them into case histories.

With writers like Ibsen and Hardy, fantasy answers impulses and needs they might not have been able to state. The truths of that fantasy we have to work out, or translate, for ourselves. With Conrad the process is reversed. We almost begin with the truths—portable truths, as it were, that can sometimes be rendered as aphorisms—and work through to their demonstration. The method was forced on him by the special circumstances that made him a writer. To understand the difficulties of this method, the extraordinary qualities of intelligence and sympathy it required, and the exercise of what he described as the "poetic faculty," we should try and look at the problem from Conrad's point of view. There is an early story which enables us to do just that.

The story is "The Return," which was written at the same time as "Karain." It is set in London and, interestingly, its two characters are English. Alvan Hervey is a City man. He is "tall, well set-up, good-looking and healthy; and his clear pale face had under its commonplace refinement that slight tinge of over-bearing brutality which is given by the possession of only partly difficult accomplishments; by excelling in games, or in the art of making money; by the easy mastery over animals and over needy men." And it is already clear that this is less a portrait than an aphorism and an idea about the middle class.

We follow Hervey home one evening. We go up to his dressing room, gaslit, with a butterfly-shaped flame coming out of the mouth of a bronze dragon. The room is full of mirrors and it is suddenly satisfactorily full of middle-class Alvan Herveys. But there is a letter on his wife's dressing table: she has left him. We follow Hervey then through every detail of his middle-class reaction: shock, nausea, humiliation, anger, sadness: paragraph after ordered paragraph, page after page. And, wonderfully, by his sheer analytical intelligence Conrad holds us.

Someone is then heard to enter the house. It is Hervey's wife: she has not, after all, had the courage to leave. What follows now is even more impressive. We move step by step with Her-vey, from the feeling of relief and triumph and the wish to pun-ish, to the conviction that the woman, a stranger after five years of marriage, "had in her hands an indispensable gift which nothing else on earth could give." So Hervey arrives at the "irresistible belief in an enigma . . . the conviction that within his reach and passing away from him was the very secret of existence—its certitude, immaterial and precious." He wants then to "compel the surrender of the gift." He tells his wife he loves her; but the shoddy words only awaken her indignation, her contempt for the "materialism" of men, and her anger at her own self-deception. Up to this point the story works. Now it fades away. Hervey remembers that his wife has not had the courage to leave; he feels that she doesn't have the "gift" which he now needs. And it is he who leaves and doesn't return.

Mysterious words are repeated in this story—"enigma," "certitude, immaterial and precious." But there is no real narrative and no real mystery. Another writer might have charted a course of events. For Conrad, though, the drama and the truth lay not in events but in the analysis: identifying the stages of consciousness through which a passionless man might move to the recognition of the importance of passion. It was the most difficult way of handling the subject; and Conrad suffered during the writing of the eighty-page story. He wrote to Edward Garnett: "It has embittered five months of my life." Such a labour; and yet, in spite of the intelligence and real perceptions, in spite of the cinematic details—the mirrors, the bronze dragon breathing fire—"The Return" remains less a story than an imaginative essay. A truth, as Conrad sees it, has been analysed. But the people remain abstractions.

And that gives another clue. The vision of middle-class people as being all alike, all consciously passionless, delightful and materialist, so that even marriage is like a conspiracy—that is the satirical vision of the outsider. The year before, when he was suffering with *The Rescue*, Conrad had written to Garnett: "Other writers have some starting point. Something to catch hold of. . . . They lean on dialect—or on tradition—or on history—or on the prejudice or fad of the hour; they trade upon some tie or conviction of their time—or upon the absence of these things—which they can abuse or praise. But at any rate they know something to begin with—while I don't. I have had some impressions, some sensations—in my time. . . . And it's all faded."

It is the complaint of a writer who is missing a society, and is beginning to understand that fantasy or imagination can move more freely within a closed and ordered world. Conrad's experience was too scattered; he knew many societies by their externals, but he knew none in depth. His human comprehension was complete. But when he set "The Return" in London he was immediately circumscribed. He couldn't risk much; he couldn't exceed his knowledge. A writer's disadvantage, when the work is done, can appear as advantages. "The Return" takes us behind the scenes early on, as it were, and gives us some idea of the necessary oddity of the work, and the prodigious labour that lay behind the novels which still stand as a meditation on our world.

It is interesting to reflect on writers' myths. With Conrad there is the imperialist myth of the man of honour, the stylist of the sea. It misses the best of Conrad, but it at least reflects the work. The myths of great writers usually have to do with their work rather than their lives. More and more today, writers' myths are about the writers themselves; the work has become less obtrusive. The great societies that produced the great novels of the past have cracked. Writing has become more private and more privately glamorous. The novel as a form no longer carries conviction. Experimentation, not aimed at the real difficulties, has corrupted response; and there is a great confusion in the minds of readers and writers about the purpose of the novel. The novelist, like the painter, no longer recognizes his interpretive function; he seeks to go beyond it; and his audience diminishes. And so the world we inhabit, which is always new, goes by unexamined, made ordinary by the camera, unmeditated on; and there is no one to awaken the sense of true wonder. That is perhaps a fair definition of the novelist's purpose, in all ages.

Conrad died fifty years ago. In those fifty years his work has penetrated to many corners of the world which he saw as dark. It is a subject for Conradian meditation; it tells us something about our new world. Perhaps it doesn't matter what we say about Conrad; it is enough that he is discussed. You will remember that for Marlow in *Heart of Darkness,* "the meaning of an episode was not inside like a kernel but outside, enveloping the tale which brought it out only as a glow brings out a haze, in the likeness of one of those misty halos that sometimes are made visible by the spectral illumination of moonshine."

July 1974

Two Worlds

(The Nobel Lecture)

THIS IS UNUSUAL for me. I have given readings and not lectures. I have told people who ask for lectures that I have no lecture to give. And that is true. It might seem strange that a man who has dealt in words and emotions and ideas for nearly fifty years shouldn't have a few to spare, so to speak. But everything of value about me is in my books. Whatever extra there is in me at any given moment isn't fully formed. I am hardly aware of it; it awaits the next book. It will—with luck—come to me during the actual writing, and it will take me by surprise. That element of surprise is what I look for when I am writing. It is my way of judging what I am doing—which is never an easy thing to do.

Proust has written with great penetration of the difference between the writer as writer and the writer as a social being. You will find his thoughts in some of his essays in *Against Sainte-Beuve,* a book reconstituted from his early papers.

The nineteenth-century French critic Sainte-Beuve believed that to understand a writer it was necessary to know as much as possible about the exterior man, the details of his life. It is a beguiling method, using the man to illuminate the work. It might seem unassailable. But Proust is able very convincingly to pick it apart. "This method of Sainte-Beuve," Proust writes, "ignores what a very slight degree of self-acquaintance teaches us: that a book is the product of a different self from the self we manifest in our habits, in our social life, in our vices. If we would try to understand that particular self, it is by searching our own bosoms, and trying to reconstruct it there, that we may arrive at it."

Those words of Proust should be with us whenever we are reading the biography of a writer—or the biography of anyone who depends on what can be called inspiration. All the details of the life and the quirks and the friendships can be laid out for us, but the mystery of the writing will remain. No amount of documentation, however fascinating, can take us there. The biography of a writer—or even the autobiography—will always have this incompleteness.

Proust is a master of happy amplification, and I would like to go back to *Against Sainte-Beuve* just for a little. "In fact," Proust writes, "it is the secretions of one's innermost self, written in solitude and for oneself alone, that one gives to the public. What one bestows on private life—in conversation . . . or in those drawing-room essays that are scarcely more than conversation in print—is the product of a quite superficial self, not of the innermost self which one can only recover by putting aside the world and the self that frequents the world."

When he wrote that, Proust had not yet found the subject that was to lead him to the happiness of his great literary labour. And you can tell from what I have quoted that he was a man trusting to his intuition and waiting for luck. I have quoted these words before in other places. The reason is that they define how I have gone about my business. I have trusted to intuition. I did it at the beginning. I do it even now. I have no idea how things might turn out, where in my writing I might go next. I have trusted to my intuition to find the subjects, and I have written intuitively. I have an idea when I start, I have a shape; but I will fully understand what I have written only after some years.

I said earlier that everything of value about me is in my books. I will go further now. I will say I am the sum of my books. Each book, intuitively sensed and, in the case of fiction, intuitively worked out, stands on what has gone before, and grows out of it. I feel that at any stage of my literary career it could have been said that the last book contained all the others.

It's been like this because of my background. My background is at once exceedingly simple and exceedingly confused. I was born in Trinidad. It is a small island in the mouth of the great Orinoco river of Venezuela. So Trinidad is not strictly of South America, and not strictly of the Caribbean. It was developed as a New World plantation colony, and when I was born in 1932 it had a population of about 400,000. Of this, about 150,000 were Indians, Hindus and Muslims, nearly all of peasant origin, and nearly all from the Gangetic plain.

This was my very small community. The bulk of this migration from India occurred after 1880. The deal was like this. People indentured themselves for five years to serve on the estates. At the end of this time they were given a small piece of land, perhaps five acres, or a passage back to India. In 1917, because of agitation by Gandhi and others, the indenture system was abolished. And perhaps because of this, or for some other reason, the pledge of land or repatriation was dishonoured for many of the later arrivals. These people were absolutely destitute. They slept in the streets of Port of Spain, the capital. When I was a child I saw them. I suppose I didn't know they were destitute—I suppose that idea came much later—and they made no impression on me. This was part of the cruelty of the plantation colony.

I was born in a small country town called Chaguanas, two or three miles inland from the Gulf of Paria. Chaguanas was a strange name, in spelling and pronunciation, and many of the Indian people—they were in the majority in the area—preferred to call it by the Indian caste name of Chauhan.

I was thirty-four when I found out about the name of my birthplace. I was living in London, had been living in England for sixteen years. I was writing my ninth book. This was a history of Trinidad, a human history, trying to re-create people and their stories. I used to go to the British Museum to read the Spanish documents about the region. These documents—recovered from the Spanish archives—were copied out for the British government in the 1890s at the time of a nasty boundary dispute with Venezuela. The documents begin in 1530 and end with the disappearance of the Spanish empire.

I was reading about the foolish search for El Dorado, and the murderous interloping of the English hero, Sir Walter Raleigh. In 1595 he raided Trinidad, killed all the Spaniards he could, and went up the Orinoco looking for El Dorado. He found nothing, but when he went back to England he said he had. He had a piece of gold and some sand to show. He said he had hacked the gold out of a cliff on the bank of the Orinoco. The Royal Mint said that the sand he asked them to assay was worthless, and other people said that he had bought the gold beforehand from North Africa. He then published a book to prove his point, and for four centuries people have believed that Raleigh had found something. The magic of Raleigh's book, which is really quite difficult to read, lay in its very long title: *The Discovery of the Large, Rich, and Beautiful Empire of Guiana, with a relation of the great and golden city of Manoa (which the Spaniards call El Dorado) and the provinces of Emeria, Aromaia, Amapaia, and other countries, with their rivers adjoining.* How real it sounds! And he had hardly been on the main Orinoco.

And then, as sometimes happens with confidence men, Raleigh was caught by his own fantasies. Twenty-one years later, old and ill, he was let out of his London prison to go to Guiana and find the gold mines he said he had found. In this fraudulent venture his son died. The father, for the sake of his reputation, for the sake of his lies, had sent his son to his death. And then Raleigh, full of grief, with nothing left to live for, went back to London to be executed.

The story should have ended there. But Spanish memories were long—no doubt because their imperial correspondence was so slow: it might take up to two years for a letter from Trinidad to be read in Spain. Eight years afterwards the Spaniards of Trinidad and Guiana were still settling their scores with the Gulf Indians. One day in the British Museum I read a letter from the King of Spain to the governor of Trinidad. It was dated 12 October 1625.

"I asked you," the King wrote, "to give me some information about a certain nation of Indians called Chaguanes, who you say number above one thousand, and are of such bad disposition that it was they who led the English when they captured the town. Their crime hasn't been punished because forces were not available for this purpose and because the Indians acknowledge no master save their own will. You have decided to give them a punishment. Follow the rules I have given you; and let me know how you get on."

What the governor did I don't know. I could find no further reference to the Chaguanes in the documents in the museum. Perhaps there were other documents about the Chaguanes in the mountain of paper in the Spanish archives in Seville which the British government scholars missed or didn't think important enough to copy out. What is true is that the little tribe of over a thousand—who would have been living on both sides of the Gulf of Paria—disappeared so completely that no one in the town of Chaguanas or Chauhan knew anything about them. And the thought came to me in the museum that I was the first person since 1625 to whom that letter of the King of Spain had a real meaning. And that letter had been dug out of the archives only in 1896 or 1897. A disappearance, and then the silence of centuries.

We lived on the Chaguanes' land. Every day in term time—I was just beginning to go to school—I walked from my grandmother's house, past the two or three main-road stores, the Chinese parlour, the Jubilee Theatre and the high-smelling little Portuguese factory that made cheap blue soap and cheap yellow soap in long bars that were put out to dry and harden in the mornings—every day I walked past these eternal-seeming things—to the Chaguanas Government School. Beyond the school was sugar-cane, estate land, going up to the Gulf of Paria. The people who had been dispossessed would have had their own kind of agriculture, their own calendar, their own codes, their own sacred sites. They would have understood the Orinoco-fed currents in the Gulf of Paria. Now all their skills and everything else about them had been obliterated.

The world is always in movement. People have everywhere at some time been dispossessed. I suppose I was shocked by this discovery in 1967 about my birthplace because I had never had any idea about it. But that was the way most of us lived in the agricultural colony, blindly. There was no plot by the authorities to keep us in our darkness. I think it was more simply that the knowledge wasn't there. The kind of knowledge about the Chaguanes would not have been considered important, and it would not have been easy to recover. They were a small tribe, and they were aboriginal. Such people—on the mainland, in what was called B.G., British Guiana—were known to us, and were a kind of joke. People who were loud and ill-behaved were known, to all groups in Trinidad, I think, as *warrahoons*. I used to think it was a made-up word, made up to suggest wildness. It was only when I began to travel in Venezuela, in my forties, that I understood that a word like that was the name of a rather large aboriginal tribe there.

There was a vague story when I was a child—and to me now it is an unbearably affecting story—that at certain times aboriginal people came across in canoes from the mainland, walked through the forest in the south of the island, and at a certain spot picked some kind of fruit or made some kind of offering, and then went back across the Gulf of Paria to the sodden estuary of the Orinoco. The rite must have been of enormous importance to have survived the upheavals of four hundred years, and the extinction of the aborigines in Trinidad. Or perhaps—though Trinidad and Venezuela have a common flora—they had come only to pick a particular kind of fruit. I don't know. I can't remember anyone inquiring. And now the memory is all lost; and that sacred site, if it existed, has become common ground.

What was past was past. I suppose that was the general attitude. And we Indians, immigrants from India, had that attitude to the island. We lived for the most part ritualised lives, and were not yet capable of self-assessment, which is where learning begins. Half of us on this land of the Chaguanes were pretending—perhaps not pretending, perhaps only feeling, never formulating it as an idea—that we had brought a kind of India with us, which we could, as it were, unroll like a carpet on the flat land.

My grandmother's house in Chaguanas was in two parts. The front part, of bricks and plaster, was painted white. It was like a kind of Indian house, with a grand balustraded terrace on the upper floor, and a prayer-room on the floor above that. It was ambitious in its decorative detail, with lotus capitals on pillars, and sculptures of Hindu deities, all done by people working only from a memory of things in India. In Trinidad it was an architectural oddity. At the back of this house, and joined to it by an upper bridge room, was a timber building in the French Caribbean style. The entrance gate was at the side, between the two houses. It was a tall gate of corrugated iron on a wooden frame. It made for a fierce kind of privacy.

So as a child I had this sense of two worlds, the world outside that tall corrugated-iron gate, and the world at home—or, at any rate, the world of my grandmother's house. It was a remnant of our caste sense, the thing that excluded and shut out. In Trinidad, where as new arrivals we were a disadvantaged community, that excluding idea was a kind of protection; it enabled us—for the time being, and only for the time being—to live in our own way and according to our own rules, to live in our own fading India. It made for an extraordinary self-centredness. We looked inwards; we lived out our days; the world outside existed in a kind of darkness; we inquired about nothing.

There was a Muslim shop next door. The little loggia of my grandmother's shop ended against his blank wall. The man's name was Mian. That was all that we knew of him and his family. I suppose we must have seen him, but I have no mental picture of him now. We knew nothing of Muslims. This idea of strangeness, of the thing to be kept outside, extended even to other Hindus. For example, we ate rice in the middle of the day, and wheat in the evenings. There were some extraordinary people who reversed this natural order and ate rice in the evenings. I thought of these people as strangers—you must imagine me at this time as under seven, because when I was seven all this life of my grandmother's house in Chaguanas came to an end for me. We moved to the capital, and then to the hills to the north-west.

But the habits of mind engendered by this shut-in and shutting-out life lingered for quite a while. If it were not for the short stories my father wrote I would have known almost nothing about the general life of our Indian community. Those stories gave me more than knowledge. They gave me a kind of solidity. They gave me something to stand on in the world. I cannot imagine what my mental picture would have been without those stories.

The world outside existed in a kind of darkness; and we inquired about nothing. I was just old enough to have some idea of the Indian epics, the *Ramayana* in particular. The children who came five years or so after me in our extended family didn't have this luck. No one taught us Hindi. Sometimes someone wrote out the alphabet for us to learn, and that was that; we were expected to do the rest ourselves. So, as English penetrated, we began to lose our language. My grandmother's house was full of religion; there were many ceremonies and readings, some of which went on for days. But no one explained or translated for us who could no longer follow the language. So our ancestral faith receded, became mysterious, not pertinent to our day-to-day life.

We made no inquiries about India or about the families people had left behind. When our ways of thinking had changed, and we wished to know, it was too late. I know nothing of the people on my father's side; I know only that some of them came from Nepal. Two years ago a kind Nepalese who liked my name sent me a copy of some pages from an 1872 gazetteer-like British work about India, *Hindu Castes and Tribes as Represented in Benares;* the pages listed—among a multitude of names—those groups of Nepalese in the holy city of Banaras who carried the name Naipal. That is all that I have.

Away from this world of my grandmother's house, where we ate rice in the middle of the day and wheat in the evenings, there was the great unknown—in this island of only 400,000 people. There were the African or African-derived people who were the majority. They were policemen; they were teachers. One of them was my very first teacher at the Chaguanas Government School; I remembered her with adoration for years. There was the capital, where very soon we would all have to go for education and jobs, and where we would settle permanently, among strangers. There were the white people, not all of them English; and the Portuguese and the Chinese, at one time also immigrants like us. And, more mysterious than these, were the people we called Spanish, *'pagnols,* mixed people of warm brown complexions who came from the Spanish time, before the island was detached from Venezuela and the Spanish empire—a kind of history absolutely beyond my child's comprehension.

To give you this idea of my background, I have had to call on knowledge and ideas that came to me much later, principally from my writing. As a child I knew almost nothing, nothing beyond what I had picked up in my grandmother's house. All children, I suppose, come into the world like that, not knowing who they are. But for the French child, say, that knowledge is waiting. That knowledge will be all around them. It will come indirectly from the conversation of their elders. It will be in the newspapers and on the radio. And at school the work of generations of scholars, scaled down for school texts, will provide some idea of France and the French.

In Trinidad, bright boy though I was, I was surrounded by areas of darkness. School elucidated nothing for me. I was crammed with facts and formulas. Everything had to be learned by heart; everything was abstract for me. Again, I do not believe there was a plan or plot to make our courses like that. What we were getting was standard school learning. In another setting it would have made sense. And at least some of the failing would have lain in me. With my limited social background it was hard for me imaginatively to enter into other societies or societies that were far away. I loved the idea of books, but I found it hard to read them. I got on best with things like Andersen and Aesop, timeless, placeless, not excluding. And when at last in the sixth form, the highest form in the college, I got to like some of our literature texts—Molière, Cyrano de Bergerac—I suppose it was because they had the quality of the fairytale.

When I became a writer those areas of darkness around me as a child became my subjects. The land; the aborigines; the New World; the colony; the history; India; the Muslim world, to which I also felt myself related; Africa; and then England, where I was doing my writing. That was what I meant when I said that my books stand one on the other, and that I am the sum of my books. That was what I meant when I said that my background, the source and prompting of my work, was at once exceedingly simple and exceedingly complicated. You will have seen how simple it was in the country town of Chaguanas. And I think you will understand how complicated it was for me as a writer. Especially in the beginning, when the literary models I had—the models given me by what I can only call my false learning—dealt with entirely different societies. But perhaps you might feel that the material was so rich it would have been no trouble at all to get started and to go on. What I have said about the background, however, comes from the knowledge I acquired with my writing. And you must believe me when I tell you that the pattern in my work has only become clear in the last two months or so. Passages from old books were read to me, and I saw the connections. Until then the greatest trouble for me was to describe my writing to people, to say what I had done.

I said I was an intuitive writer. That was so, and that remains so now, when I am nearly at the end. I never had a plan. I followed no system. I worked intuitively. My aim every time was to do a book, to create something that would be easy and interesting to read. At every stage I could only work within my knowledge and sensibility and talent and world view. Those things developed book by book. And I had to do the books I did because there were no books about those subjects to give me what I wanted. I had to clear up my world, elucidate it, for myself.

I had to go to the documents in the British Museum and elsewhere, to get the true feel of the history of the colony. I had to travel to India because there was no one to tell me what the India my grandparents had come from was like. There was the writing of Nehru and Gandhi; and strangely it was Gandhi, with his South African experience, who gave me more, but not enough. There was Kipling; there were British-Indian writers like John Masters (going very strong in the 1950s, with an announced plan, later abandoned, I fear, for thirty-five connected novels about British India); there were romances by women writers. The few Indian writers who had come up at that time were middle-class people, town-dwellers; they didn't know the India we had come from.

And when that Indian need was satisfied, others became apparent: Africa, South America, the Muslim world. The aim has always been to fill out my world picture, and the purpose comes from my childhood: to make me more at ease with myself. Kind people have sometimes written asking me to go and write about Germany, say, or China. But there is much good writing already about those places; I am willing to depend there on the writing that exists. And those subjects are for other people. Those were not the areas of darkness I felt about me as a child. So, just as there is a development in my work, a development in narrative skill and knowledge and sensibility, so there is a kind of unity, a focus, though I might appear to be going in many directions.

When I began I had no idea of the way ahead. I wished only to do a book. I was trying to write in England, where I stayed on after my years at the university, and it seemed to me that my experience was very thin, was not truly of the stuff of books. I could find in no book anything that came near my background. The young French or English person who wished to write would have found any number of models to set him on his way. I had none. My father's stories about our Indian community belonged to the past. My world was quite different. It was more urban, more mixed. The simple physical details of the chaotic life of our extended family—sleeping rooms or sleeping spaces, eating times, the sheer number of people—seemed impossible to handle. There was too much to be explained, both about my home life and about the world outside. And at the same time there was also too much about us—like our own ancestry and history—that I didn't know.

At last one day there came to me the idea of starting with the Port of Spain street to which we had moved from Chaguanas. There was no big corrugated-iron gate shutting out the world there. The life of the street was open to me. It was an intense pleasure for me to observe it from the verandah. This street life was what I began to write about. I wished to write fast, to avoid too much self-questioning, and so I simplified. I suppressed the child-narrator's background. I ignored the racial and social complexities of the street. I explained nothing. I stayed at ground level, so to speak. I presented people only as they appeared on the street. I wrote a story a day. The first stories were very short. I was worried about the material lasting long enough. But then the writing did its magic. The material began to present itself to me from many sources. The stories became longer; they couldn't be written in a day. And then the inspiration, which at one stage had seemed very easy, rolling me along, came to an end. But a book had been written, and I had in my own mind become a writer.

The distance between the writer and his material grew with the two later books; the vision was wider. And then intuition led me to a large book about our family life. During this book my writing ambition grew. But when it was over I felt I had done all that I could do with my island material. No matter how much I meditated on it, no further fiction would come.

Accident, then, rescued me. I became a traveller. I travelled in the Caribbean region and understood much more about the colonial set-up of which I had been part. I went to India, my ancestral land, for a year; it was a journey that broke my life in two. The books that I wrote about these two journeys took me to new realms of emotion, gave me a world view I had never had, extended me technically. I was able in the fiction that then came to me to take in England as well as the Caribbean—and how hard that was to do. I was able also to take in all the racial groups of the island, which I had never before been able to do.

This new fiction was about colonial shame and fantasy, a book, in fact, about how the powerless lie about themselves, and lie to themselves, since it is their only resource. The book was called *The Mimic Men*. And it was not about mimics. It was about colonial men mimicking the condition of manhood, men who had grown to distrust everything about themselves. Some pages of this book were read to me the other day—I hadn't looked at it for more than thirty years—and it occurred to me that I had been writing about colonial schizophrenia. But I hadn't thought of it like that. I had never used abstract words to describe any writing purpose of mine. If I had, I would never have been able to do the book. The book was done intuitively, and only out of close observation.

I have done this little survey of the early part of my career to try to show the stages by which, in just ten years, my birthplace had altered or developed in my writing: from the comedy of street life to a study of a kind of widespread schizophrenia. What was simple had become complicated.

Both fiction and the travel-book form have given me my way of looking; and you will understand why for me all literary forms are equally valuable. It came to me, for instance, when I set out to write my third book about India—twenty-six years after the first—that what was most important about a travel book were the people the writer travelled among. The people had to define themselves. A simple enough idea, but it required a new kind of book; it called for a new way of travelling. And it was the very method I used later when I went, for the second time, into the Muslim world.

I have always moved by intuition alone. I have no system, literary or political. I have no guiding political idea. I think that probably lies with my ancestry. The Indian writer R. K. Narayan, who died this year, had no political idea. My father, who wrote his stories in a very dark time, and for no reward, had no political idea. Perhaps it is because we have been far from authority for many centuries. It gives us a special point of view. I feel we are more inclined to see the humour and pity of things.

Nearly thirty years ago I went to Argentina. It was at the time of the guerrilla crisis. People were waiting for the old dictator Perón to come back from exile. The country was full of hate. Peronists were waiting to settle old scores. One such man said to me, "There is good torture and bad torture." Good torture was what you did to the enemies of the people. Bad torture was what the enemies of the people did to you. People on the other side were saying the same thing. There was no true debate about anything. There was only passion and the borrowed political jargon of Europe. I wrote, "Where jargon turns living issues into abstractions, and where jargon ends by competing with jargon, people don't have causes. They only have enemies."

And the passions of Argentina are still working themselves out, still defeating reason and consuming lives. No resolution is in sight.

I am near the end of my work now. I am glad to have done what I have done, glad creatively to have pushed myself as far as I could go. Because of the intuitive way in which I have written, and also because of the baffling nature of my material, every book has come as a blessing. Every book has amazed me; up to the moment of writing I never knew it was there. But the greatest miracle for me was getting started. I feel—and the anxiety is still vivid to me—that I might easily have failed before I began.

I will end as I began, with one of the marvellous little essays of Proust in *Against Sainte-Beuve*. "The beautiful things we shall write if we have talent," Proust says, "are inside us, indistinct, like the memory of a melody which delights us though we are unable to recapture its outline. Those who are obsessed by this blurred memory of truths they have never known are the men who are gifted. . . . Talent is like a sort of memory which will enable them finally to bring this indistinct music closer to them, to hear it clearly, to note it down. . . ."

Talent, Proust says. I would say luck, and much labour.

2001

Index

CREDITS

Some of the essays in this work have been previously published in the following:

"Conrad's Darkness and Mine": *New York Review of Books* (1974)

"East Indian": *The Reporter* (7 June 1965), and subsequently in *The Overcrowded Barracon* (André Deutsch, 1972)

"Foreword to *The Adventures of Gurudeva*": *The Adventures of Gurudeva* (André Deutsch, June 1975)

"Foreword to *A House for Mr. Biswas*": *A House for Mr. Biswas* (Alfred A. Knopf, 1983)

"Indian Autobiographies": *New Statesman* (29 January 1965), and subsequently in *The Overcrowded Barracon* (André Deutsch, 1972)

"Jasmine": *The Times Literary Supplement* (4 June 1964), and subsequently in *The Overcrowded Barracon* (André Deutsch, 1972)

"The Last of the Aryans": *Encounter* (January 1966), and subsequently in *The Overcrowded Barracon* (André Deutsch, 1972)

"Prologue to an Autobiography": *Finding the Center* (Alfred A. Knopf, 1984)

"Reading and Writing, a Personal Account": *New York Review of Books* (1999)

"Theatrical Natives": *New Statesman* (2 December 1966), and subsequently in *The Overcrowded Barracon* (André Deutsch, 1972)

"Two Worlds (the Nobel Lecture)": 7 December 2001 (www.nobel.se/literature/laureate/2001/naipaul-lecture-e.html)

picador.com

blog
videos
interviews
extracts